Catastrophe
or
Cornucopia

Catastrophe
or
Cornucopia

The Environment, Politics and the Future

Stephen Cotgrove

Professor of Sociology, University of Bath

1807 1982

JOHN WILEY & SONS

Chichester · New York · Brisbane · Toronto · Singapore

Library of Congress Cataloging in Publication Data:

Cotgrove, Stephen, F.
   Catastrophe or cornucopia.

   Bibliography: p.
   Includes index.
   1. Environmental policy.   I. Title.
HC79.E5C668   363.7'5   81-14827

ISBN 0 471 10079 X

British Library Cataloguing in Publication Data:

Cotgrove, Stephen
   Catastrophe or cornucopia.
   1. Human ecology
   2. Environmental policy
   I. Title
   304.2   GF41

ISBN 0 471 10079 X (cloth)
      0 471 10166 4 (paper)

Phototypeset by Dobbie Typesetting Service, Plymouth, Devon, England
and printed in the United States of America.

Preface

Social scientists are not very good at anticipating change. Student unrest in the 1960s, and the more widespread and even dramatic increase in direct action across a wide spectrum caught most by surprise. Looking back, the complacency of the late 1950s and early 1960s was ill-founded. Almond and Verba's influential study celebrated the stability of pluralist democracy, rooted in a civic culture marked by high levels of confidence in political processes and institutions. Yet within a year or two of its publication, there were signs of the coming storm. All this has changed. Marches, rallies, rent strikes, disruption of public inquiries, sit-ins—are all indications of a marked crisis of confidence in politics. And environmental issues—motorways, urban redevelopment, reservoirs, airports, and nuclear installations—have been the focus for the expression of various forms of 'outsider' politics.

Does the last decade mark a turning point in the history of industrialization? Or are recent events a temporary perturbation in the onward march of progress towards a future of plenty in which affluence will have dissolved the traditional causes of political conflict? Will the future be shaped by the inexorable march of technology? Is the spring which drives industrial society weakening—the pursuit of material goals and satisfactions? Is there a change in values—in support for post-material or post-acquisitive goals? What kind of future do people want? And is the political system adapted to cope with change?

The rise of the environmentalist movement is but one example of a growth in public interest groups which in various ways challenge economic individualism and the market ideology. The levelling off in economic growth sharpens the awareness of conflict between wealth production and welfare. The energy crisis and emerging shortages of some essential raw materials are eroding the buoyant optimism of a decade ago and lending an element of credence to what was dismissed as doomsday alarmism. In short, there is not only evidence of a crisis of confidence in the business civilization, but signs that it may be threatened as its very foundations—its ability to satisfy receding horizons of material expectation.

v

Against this background, the vision of a benign post-industrial society looks increasingly unconvincing. Like most utopian thought, the post-industrial society thesis is strangely silent on the politics of change. The politics of a post-industrial society, especially one faced with intransigent economic problems, could well be far from benign. The increasing demands for real participation and involvement, plus a growing reaction against the more negative and threatening aspects of technology could put an intolerable strain on democratic processes. The various responses of governments to opposition to nuclear power are the writing on the wall. If this book has one central message, it is to raise questions about the political perception of the strains facing all industrial societies, and the adequacy of the political response.

The researches on environmentalists reported here provide a case study for the exploration of such wider issues. The environmentalist movement has provided a focus for the expressions of discontents with many of the central features of industrial society—centralization, a growing sense of helplessness in the face of impersonal bureaucracies, and the growing influence of experts in decisions involving complex technology. Environmentalists do not share in the dominant faith—in science and technology, and in the economic individualism of the market place (Chapters 2–4). Their beliefs and values are in sharp contrast to those of the dominant industrialists. Indeed, environmentalists and industrialists face each other uncomprehendingly, the blind talking to the deaf, each accusing the other of irrationality. The political consequences are worrying and pose challenging questions about the adequacy of political processes to cope with what are certain to be continuing conflicts over nuclear installations, roads, dams and airports. If it were only a handful of environmentalists, then the problem would not perhaps be so threatening. But against the background of evidence of a more widespread crisis of confidence and a decline in the legitimacy of politics, the prognosis is worrying.

Social scientists do not possses a crystal ball which enables them to foretell the future. But they can try to do better than in the past by anticipating short term change. And central to any understanding of change is the values and goals to which groups in society attach importance and which they come to define as a basis for legitimate political demands. This study of environmentalists hopefully increases our understanding of the marked generational changes in values which have been observed in all advanced industrial society, and which could present political systems with strains for which they are ill-prepared.

Acknowledgements

It is always invidious to attempt to identify those who have contributed significantly to any intellectual enterprise. I am especially indebted to the Social Science Research Council whose grant made the research possible, and to the Institute for Environment and Society, Berlin, for the stimulus of collaboration in an international comparative survey, and for additional funds to assist later stages of the fieldwork. The week spent with Nicholas Watts, Joachim Fietkau and Lester Milbrath was both stimulating and a source of new and valuable insights. Thanks also to those who gave so generously of their time by completing questionnaires.

I am especially grateful too, to the Nuffield Foundation and the University of Bath who made possible a memorable series of visits to universities and research centres in the U.S.A. To Mary Douglas (Russell Sage Foundation, New York), Lester Milbrath (SUNY, Buffalo), Dorothy Nelkin and Fred Buttell (Cornell), Riley Dunlap and Bill Catton (Washington State), Richard Gale (Oregon), Aaron Wildavsky and Dr. Tannenbaum (Berkeley, California) I am especially grateful. But my indebtedness goes beyond to those many individuals who listened, argued, made available material both published and unpublished, and gave freely of their time. The warmth of their welcome is unforgettable. The extensive citation of American studies is some indication of the extent of my indebtedness.

I owe a special debt to Andrew Duff, Research Officer on the project. His background in the natural sciences brought new perspectives to the analysis. The construction of the questionnaire and the statistical analysis owe a great deal to his expertise. The development of models and theoretical perspectives was a genuinely collaborative effort.

I am grateful to *The Sociological Review, British Journal of Sociology*, George Allen and Unwin, and the Manchester University Press for permission to include previously published material, to *American Studies* and Riley Dunlap for permission to include extracts in Chapter 1.

viii

Last, but by no means least, I wish to express sincere thanks to Elizabeth Sherrard for expertly typing the manuscript, and patiently piecing together changes and revisions as the book took shape.

STEPHEN COTGROVE
University of Bath

Contents

CHAPTER 1

Catastrophe or Cornucopia

'The principal defect of the industrial way of life with its ethos of expansion is that it is not sustainable . . . . We can be certain . . . that sooner or later it will end . . . whether against our will, in a succession of famines, epidemics, social crises and wars; or because we want it to . . .' (Goldsmith *et al.*, 1972 p.15).

These are the opening words from an issue of the *Ecologist* devoted entirely to the presentation of *A Blueprint for Survival*, subsequently published as a Penguin Special. The *Sunday Times* reviewer described it as 'nightmarishly convincing . . . after reading it nothing seems quite the same any more'. In the same year, the so-called Club of Rome had published its *Limits to Growth* (Meadows *et al.* 1972). But these were only a part of a flood of reports, books and articles, which came to be referred to somewhat disparagingly as the prophets of doom. All had in common the same message—that the industrial world could not go on as it was; that continued exponential economic growth was a physical impossibility, and that growth in population, pollution, production, the use of energy and non-renewable resources had reached a point where, unless drastic action was taken, crisis and collapse was inevitable. The reaction was swift. John Maddox (1972), former editor of *Nature*, published a strong attack and refutation of the 'doomsday syndrome', while a team at the University of Sussex produced a scholarly and authoritative critique of the Club of Rome report.

THE 'NEW' ENVIRONMENTALISM

Why then did the environment erupt into consciousness at this time? Why the upsurge of new environmentalist associations in the 1960s? There is nothing new, of course, about environmental concern (Sinclair 1973). Indeed, the growth of public interest groups promoting some aspect of environmental protection goes back to the 1890s (Table 1.1). The National Trust, with a membership approaching one million, was founded in 1895; the Ramblers' Association in 1925, and the Youth Hostels Association in 1930. In the

1

U.S.A., one of the most influential and successful, the Sierra Club, similarly dates from 1892, while the largest, the National Wildlife Foundation with 620 000 members, began in 1936. Over the last decade, support has probably doubled, so that now there are between two and a half and three million members, about one in ten of the adult population (Lowe *et al.* 1980).

Such a list makes it abundantly clear that environmental groups embrace a very wide diversity of interests and approaches, from the preservation of wildlife and the national heritage of buildings, to the enjoyment of the countryside through rambling, hostelling and caravanning. Such a broad based movement attracting so much support is undoubtedly of importance. But the groups which formed in the late 1960s and early 1970s took on a new

Table 1.1. Public interest environmental groups in the United Kingdom (as at 1979/80)

Name	Date of Founding	Membership
Established Groups		
Commons, Open Spaces and Footpaths Preservation Society (1)	1865	3,000
Society for the Protection of Ancient Buildings	1877	5,000
Royal Society for the Protection of Birds	1889	300,000
National Trust	1895	1,000,000
Town and Country Planning Association	1899	2,000
Royal Society for Nature Conservation	1912	129,000
Ancient Monuments Society	1924	2,000
Council for the Protection of Rural England	1926	31,000
Youth Hostels Association	1930	294,000
Ramblers Association	1935	32,000
Georgian Group	1937	2,000
Soil Association	1946	5,000
Civic Trust (2)	1957	300,000
Victorian Society	1958	3,000 (est.)
New Groups		
Conservation Society	1966	6,000
Co En Co (3)	1969	—
Friends of the Earth	1970	15,000 (est.)
Socialist Environmental Resources Association	1973	700
Ecology Party	1973	4,500
Conservative Ecology Group	1977	300
Liberal Ecology Group	1977	300

(1) This includes 2,000 ordinary members and 1,000 local authorities as members.
(2) This figure represents the membership of groups registered with the Trust.
(3) Co En Co, the Committee for Environmental Conservation is a coalition of non-governmental organisations acting as a central coordinating body of three — the other two are the Liberal Ecology Group and the Conservative Ecology Group. (There is in addition the Ecology Party.)

Taken from a survey conducted by Philip Lowe and Jane Goyder to be fully reported in their book *Environmental Groups in British Politics* (George Allen and Unwin, 1982).

and distinctive direction. The Friends of the Earth and the Conservation Society in Britain, and Environmental Defense and Environmental Action in the U.S.A. are all examples of groups who sought a more direct political impact. Most important, their message was that environmental catastrophe could be avoided only by fundamental and radical changes in the values and institutions of industrial societies.[1] And it is with this new dimension to environmentalism that this study is concerned.

To understand its significance, we need a clearer picture of the essential elements in the new environmentalism.[2] If there is one message which rings out bold and clear in its early phase, it is the warning of limits to the ability of the earth to sustain the present levels of economic and population growth, consumption of resources, and the destruction of the ecosphere through pollution and agricultural methods. The writings of Forrester and the Club of Rome exerted a powerful influence. The root of the crisis was diagnosed to be exponential growth (Meadows *et al.* 1972). World population, for example, is doubling every 35 years. This means that the present level of population, which has taken the total length of human history to achieve, will be doubled in an incredibly short space of time. Although a doubling in size is supportable when the values are small, from 8 to 16, or 64 to 128, beyond a certain value increases come to be beyond the capacity of the system to support them. And this, it is argued, is the stage which the world industrial systems have now reached. Hence, catastrophe by the year 2000 is inevitable through the exhaustion of resources, and rising death rates from pollution and food shortages, unless urgent steps are taken to reverse the trend. A range of possible changes are explored in turn, including technological advances to control pollution, the discovery of new sources of energy and increased food supply. The possibility of any technological fix to avert rather than simply postpone catastrophe is ruled out. The analysis of *Limits* leads inexorably to the conclusion that the only possibility of salvation lies in recognizing the limits to economic and population growth and working towards a stable world population and steady state economy: in short, a state of global equilibrium. And because population growth and growth in industrial output are both exponential, it is a matter of extreme urgency to change direction this decade. This is especially true of population because of the lag between reductions in fertility and a decline in the rate of growth.

Before the end of the year which had seen the publication of the *Blueprint for Survival* and the *Limits to Growth*, John Maddox's (1972) counter attack was in print.[3] His rejection of the environmentalist case was threefold. Firstly, Maddox argued, they have grossly exaggerated the problems. Secondly, they have ignored or brushed aside evidence which gives grounds for optimism, and have focused entirely on the most gloomy evidence. Thirdly, in their denigration of science and technology as the source of many of our environmental problems they have not only mistakenly blamed technology for what are often administrative errors, but have thrown away the one tool which offers promise of amelioration or cure.

More specifically on food supplies Maddox is optimistic:

There is a good chance that the problems of the 1970s and 1980s will not be famine and starvation but, ironically, the problems of how best to dispose of food surpluses in countries where famine has until recently been endemic. (Maddox 1972, p.3).

His optimism stems from the steady record of success in improving plant yields (the 'green revolution'), and the fact that in some areas in recent years the increase in output comfortably exceeds rapid population growth. Similarly, he is quite confident that despite considerable growth in demand, there will be no energy gap. Although petroleum reserves will last only about 135 years, rising prices will ensure their replacement by fresh sources:

All fears of fuel shortages should in any case have been dispelled by the coming nuclear power, which has already broadened the range of choice . . . . The prospect, always unrealistically dramatic, of a crippling scarcity of energy has been exorcised by a single technological development. (Maddox 1972 p.84).

There were other influential attacks and refutations. The University of Sussex's study focused especially on fundamental weaknesses in the methodology of the *Limits* analysis. The entire argument rests on the extrapolation of exponential growth, and it was this which was criticized by the Sussex study:

It does not require a sophisticated computed analysis to realise that if the assumption is made that threatening trends increase exponentially while negative feedback loops increase only arithmetically, catastrophe must occur at some point. (Jahoda 1973 p.210).

In short, it was argued, there is a failure to take sufficient account of the human adaptation to situations. Previous forecasts of exponential population growth have proved wrong, because they failed to recognize the human response to declining mortality resulting in deliberate attempts to limit family size. This is one example of the underestimation of negative feedback loops, that might 'bend the imaginary exponential growth curves to gentler slopes than "overshoot and collapse"' (Jahoda 1973 p.211).[4]

Controversy has raged then across a variety of specific issues, the pollution of lakes and rivers, the exhaustion of non-renewable resources of minerals and fuel, the inability of the planet to support population growth, climatic changes through the use of fossil fuels for energy and through de-forestation, health threats through the entry of pesticides in food chains, and the destruction of the protective ozone layer by the use of aerosols. For the new environmentalists, these and other issues are all symptomatic of faulty relations with our environment. And these are all seen to be rooted in our growth-oriented society.

But warnings of an impending crisis from exceeding the earth's carrying capacity is only half the message. Both the *Blueprint* and the pages of the *Ecologist* are explicit about the sources of the crisis and its implications for social change. Both are eloquent in their praise of small self-sufficient decentralized communities. Growth, it is argued, is not only the root cause of pollution, the instability of the ecosystem, and the depletion of resources. Growth is also at the root cause of the breakdown of contemporary society judged by a series of indicators of social pathology. It is the crowded tenements and the large cities which are the breeding grounds of delinquency and broken homes.

'We have seen that man in our present society has been deprived of a satisfactory social environment. A society made of decentralised, self-sufficient communities, in which people work near their homes, have the responsibility of governing themselves, of running their schools, hospitals and welfare services, in fact of constituting real communities, would we feel be a much happier place. Its members, in these conditions, would be likely to develop an identity of their own, which many of us have lost in the mass society we live in. They would tend, once more, to find an aim in life, develop a set of values, and take pride in their achievements as well as in those of their community.

It is the absence of just these things that is rendering our mass society ever less tolerable to us and in particular to our youth, and to which can be attributed the present rise in drug addiction, alcoholism and delinquency, all of which are symptomatic of a social disease in which a society fails to furnish its members with their basic psychological requirements.' (*Blueprint for Survival* p.62).

The new environmentalists are agreed on the need for fundamental social change if society is to survive. But there the consensus evaporates. On closer examination, basic differences emerge which make it possible to construct two major variations of the new enviromentalism—a traditional and a radical form (Cotgrove 1976). The traditional form, exemplified specifically by the *Blueprint* and by many articles in the *Ecologist*, sees the return to small-scale decentralized communities as the only way to halt the growing disintegration and disorder of mass industrial society. But the emphasis is on the restoration of order, based on what is seen to be the natural order of the close-knit community.[5]

This emphasis on order and traditional authority emerging from the will of the community is forcefully expressed in Garret Hardin's (1968) much quoted paper 'The Tragedy of the Commons'. Here he concludes that some freedoms such as the freedom to breed are intolerable. Far from being a dirty word, coercion is essential. But it is the coercion of the collective will:

To many, the word coercion implies arbitrary decisions of distant and unresponsible bureaucrats: but this is not a necessary part of its meaning. The only kind of coercion I recommend is mutual coercion, mutually agreed upon by the majority of the people affected.

Radical environmentalists, by contrast, are attracted to small-scale self-sufficient communities by their promise of personal autonomy, and escape from the restrictions of hierarchical and bureaucratic structures. An important element in the anti-nuclear power movement is growing opposition to state power (Touraine 1979). Some, especially the younger students attracted to the movement, go further and are inspired by the anarchist ideals of Kropotkin and Godwin, seeking a society in which power and authority is no longer a necessary part (Bookchin 1974):

Ecology activists are not concerned with power: at least they are anarchists, like the underground people. They have no wish to take political or economic power from one section of society and give it to another section. They are not Marxist. . . . The revolution in this sense is much more akin to a religious conversion "a turning about at the seat of consciousness". ' (Allaby 1971, p.76).

The second dimension on which there is polarization is around questions of differentiation and equality. The traditional form justifies inequality, competition and hierarchy by appeals to the natural order:

Undifferentiated individuals competing for the same ecological niche cannot cooperate in any way . . . . It is only when as a result of competition, they have been found to specialise in such a way that each one learns to exploit a different sub-niche, that cooperation is possible . . .'.

'Competition is a means whereby a hierarchy is set up. In the right conditions . . . the competing individuals eventually arrange themselves so as to constitute a hierarchy and learn to accept their respective positions within this hierarchy' (Goldsmith 1974, p.125).

Competition also justifies irregularities of reward:

'The heritage of wilderness must be open only to those who can earn it again for themselves. The rest, since they cannot gain the genuine treasure by their own efforts, must relinquish the shadow of it.' (Hardin 1968).

On a third polarity, attitudes towards scientific modes of thought, the two forms of environmentalism have more in common. Both are critical towards science and technology and the belief that the contemporary crisis can be solved by some kind of 'technological fix'. Some go further and blame reductionist science[6] for the mess. Hence the attraction of ecology to environmentalists. This branch of biology studies systems of animals and plants in relation to their habitats. It has particular appeal because it stresses the interrelations and interdependence between all life forms, and the one-ness of nature. Both forms of environmentalism agree on the inadequacies and limits of a reductionist and mechanistic science. But whereas the radical form uses such arguments to promote the liberation of man, traditional utopianism is more likely to seek justification for forms of social control in the more mystical notions of Nature, 'blood and soil', and the group will.[7]

There is an exception: the alternative technology movement differs from other expressions of radical enviromentalism. Although it is basically anarchistic, and favours self-sufficient communes as a means of resisting the centralizing bureaucratic trends in industrial society, it rejects neither science nor technology. It is not technology *per se* which is seen to be repressive, but only the forms which technology has taken — harnessed to the objectives of a repressive society. The search is for alternative 'soft' technologies which facilitate independence from centrally controlled services — small-scale systems for localised energy and communications, and self-sufficient living (Harper 1974; Dickson 1974).[8]

CORNUCOPIAN ENVIRONMENTALISTS

What the new enviromentalists have in common is their opposition to industrialization. But there is one major variation that is not anti-industraliza-tion, but is opposed only to the capitalist mode of production, and is rooted in a Marxist critique of capitalism (Commoner 1972; Rothman 1972; Enzensberger 1974; Beresford 1977). The crux of their case is that it is the exploitative and predatory nature of capitalism which is at the root of the current environmental crisis. It is the destructive powers unleashed by capitalism which threatens our survival (Enzensberger 1974, p.31). They share with other environmentalists the view that industrial societies are heading for disaster if they go on as they are. But their outlook is essentially cornucopian. In the *Closing Circle* (1972) Barry Commoner argues that the root cause of the coming crisis is to be found in faulty technologies. He provides evidence to show that economic growth since World War II (in both socialist and capitalist societies), has been characterized mainly by new technologies which replace natural products, such as wool and cotton, with high-energy consuming and ecologically damaging products such as plastics and man-made fibres. The thrust towards such developments is to be found in the imperatives to maximize profits and productivity. The solution to the environmental crisis is therefore to be located primarily in a change in the relations of production. In *The Poverty of Power* (1976) Commoner develops the same line of argument:

There is enough petroleum in the United States to meet all our needs for the next fifty years. There is no evidence that physical limitations on our ability to produce cotton and wool have led to the production of synthetics that consume petroleum resources so wastefully; . . . or that we must produce detergents because there is not enough fat to make all the needed soap. . . . In each case, they are brought about not by some abstract mindless force called "growth", but by deliberate human actions motivated by an *economic* factor — the desire to maximise profits.'

A somewhat similar argument is put forward by Tanzer (1974):

. . . there is no real energy crisis in the sense of a physical shortage of energy resources; rather, there is an artificially contrived scarcity, generated by various forces operating with the overall framework of the international capitalist economy.' (Tanzer 1974, p.11).

Despite their differences, what unites the environmentalists is their criticism of many of the central features of modern industrial societies. It is for this reason that we can speak of 'utopian environmentalism', not in any pejorative sense as some unattainable dream, but in the sense that the new environmentalism is rooted in a moral critique of industrial capitalism, and seeks to promote an alternative version of the good society.

ENVIRONMENTALIST MOVEMENT

If by social movements we mean those forms of collective behaviour which are relatively unstructured, self-conscious attempts 'to introduce innovations into a social system' (Banks 1972), then it is this which differentiates the new environmentalism of the 1960s. In its early days, the movement was marked by the messianic fervour of its message. If mankind was to be saved, the change must be radical: piecemeal tinkering would not suffice. The preface to the *Blueprint* claims to herald 'the formation of the MOVEMENT FOR SURVIVAL . . . and, it is hoped, the dawn of a new age in which man will learn to live with the rest of Nature rather than against it.' Ann Chisholm (1972) has recorded similar impressions. Following the interest generated by Sir Frank Fraser Darling's Reith lectures in 1969, her investigations included interviews with a number of distinguished 'ecologists':

'What interested me, first of all, was not the actual content of ecology but the ecological message. Here, it seemed, was a new morality and a strategy for human survival rolled into one . . . . During the autumn of 1969, ecology caught on like a new religion among the young on college campuses across the country . . . (the ecologists) could, it seemed, offer a general philosophy of life that explained man's dependence upon, and responsibility towards nature . . . . In an increasingly directionless, secular world, the intricate patterns traced by the ecologists offered a potential source of comfort, a sense of the unity and beauty of life.' (Chisholm 1972, pp.xi–xii).

Commenting on one of Ehrlich's meetings which she attended, Anne Chisholm reports:

He had the audience gripped and it struck me that there was more than a touch of the revivalist technique in his accusatory style, in the way he brought home to his eager listeners their own guilt and complicity.' (Chisholm 1972, pp.142–3).

There is little doubt that what triggered the movement and raised the level of public consciousness was the combination of influential publications, including notably Rachel Carson's *Silent Spring* (1965) and the report of the Club of Rome, backed by dramatic events such as the eutrophication of Lake Erie, and the mercury poisoning of Lake Minimata in Japan. But such events are not themselves enough to explain the emergence of an environmentalist movement. Nor was a growing awareness of environmental problems confined to industrial capitalist countries of the West. In the U.S.S.R., an emerging conflict between the pursuit of industrial growth and environmental degradation was becoming apparent in the 1960s. There was growing evidence that planned developments in the paper and pulp industries on the shores of Lake Baikal threatened irreversible damage to the lake's ecosystems. But the initial opposition of scientists and the publication and dissemination of information was suppressed. Komarov (1978) argues that in fact there is evidence of widespread environmental problems. In a carefully documented case he draws attention to marked increases in lung cancer and genetic defects. Moreover, although the Soviet Union has set rigorous standards for maximum permissible concentrations, these are almost everywhere exceeded by factors of up to 100 in the pollution of air and water.

In its early stages, the new environmentalism won widespread popular support, and clocked up impressive legislative gains, particularly in the U.S.A., where its youthful supporters were drawn from the ranks of those who had sympathized with the range of radical student concerns of the late 1960s (Buttel 1980). There was early optimism that the goal of environmental quality would soon be achieved. Indeed, there appeared to be a widespread consensus that cleaning up the environment was in everyone's interest, and that all were agreed on the desirability of clean air and water (Dunlap 1976). The movement has now lost much of its momentum, and has been forced increasingly into defending its gains against mounting attack. Part of the explanation is the effect of economic conditions. It is significant that each of the periods of growth, in the 1890s, 1920s, late 1950s and early 1970s, occurred towards the end of periods of sustained economic growth (Lowe *et al.* 1980). Economic stagnation together with the energy crisis have resulted in a growing questioning of environmental policies:

'Environmentalists are reeling in the wake of massive sentiments that environmental controls must be relaxed in order to hasten delivery of more energy from coal fields and oil shales, and to expedite the deployment of nuclear power plants.' (Buttel 1980).

It is also argued that the early success of the movement generated organized opposition, a 'counter-movement', an ecological backlash from those whose interests were threatened and on whose shoulders fell the burden and cost of reform (Albrecht 1972). The opposition has made much of the threat to jobs and to economic growth. In short, opposition is explained in terms of costs and benefits.

A more fundamental explanation argues that the roots of opposition are to be found in the lack of congruence between the goals of the environmentalist movement and the values of the wider society. American researches are almost unanimous in identifying as important: personal freedom, individual rights, democracy, equal opportunity, achievement, success, material comfort and progress; plus (less unanimously) free enterprise, private property, nationalism, and science and technology. Environmental quality is notably absent. The closest approximation is 'a world of beauty' included by Rokeach (1973) which ranked low (15 out of 18) in his list of terminal values. Efforts to achieve environmental quality pose a direct threat to cherished values: to individual freedoms, property rights, free enterprise, and material comforts (Dunlap 1976).[9]

As a result, it is argued, the environmentalist movement has been forced to change from a consensual to a conflictual movement, from a concern with reform within a framework of consensual values to a radical challenge to societal values. In Smelser's (1962) terminology, this is the change from a norm-oriented to a value-oriented movement (Dunlap 1976).[10] Following the first Earth Day (22 April 1970), the dominant thrust of the movement in the U.S.A. was to work for new regulatory agencies and laws. But despite considerable success there has been a growing realization that problems such as water pollution and wild-life preservation continue to worsen. Consequently, there has been a change in the goals of the movement to a growing emphasis on the need for more fundamental changes in basic societal values. This has been accompanied by a change in strategies. In the early phase, there was an emphasis on a strategy of 'personal transformation'; of changing individual behaviour through recycling efforts and purchasing environmentally safe products. This was followed in subsequent years by a shift towards societal manipulation, with an increasing emphasis on legal action against polluters and various direct forms of action. This shift from personal transformation to power tactics, argues Dunlap (1976), owes much to the growing realization of a fundamental conflict between the values and goals of the environmentalist movement and the dominant societal values.

This is, of course, an oversimplification. The movement has always included a mixture of reformers and radicals; of those whose strategy is to change the individual and of those who seek a radical change in the social system. What Dunlap is arguing is that the dynamics of the movement, resulting from an emerging conflict with dominant societal values, is pushing it in the direction of more radical strategies (Figure 1.1). The importance of the theory is that it provides a framework for identifying a series of researchable issues. In particular, it underlines the crucial question of the extent to which the values of the new environmentalism are in opposition to the dominant social values. This is central to any exploration of the social and political significance of the enviromentalist movement.

To analyse the various threads of social criticism and dissent which interweave within a broad environmental consciousness may give a false picture of tidy and consistent positions. What we have identified are the major themes which emerge from a wide study of environmentalist publications and pronouncements, and of available researches. The existence of any coherent environmentalist ideology or ideologies within the minds of identifiable groups of environmentalists can only be discovered by empirical research among the

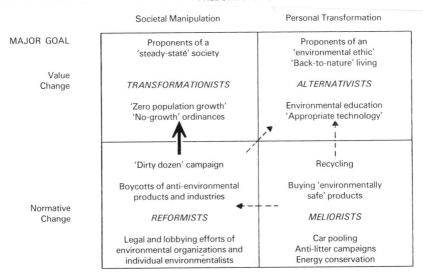

PREDOMINANT STRATEGY

Figure 1.1. A typology for mapping the changing environmental movement.* From Dunlap, 1976. Paper presented at the Society for the Study of Social Problems, held in New York, August 1976

*Adapted from Aberle, 1966; Smelser, 1962; and Turner and Killian, 1972. Arrows indicate hypothesized major (solid line) and minor (dotted line) directions of shifts from 1970 to the present.

membership. This we have attempted, and we report our findings in subsequent chapters.

SOCIAL ROOTS OF ENVIRONMENTALISM

If social movements are attempts to change the social system, they can only be understood within the context of the societies they seek to change. Although we have stressed the distinctive character of the new 'utopian' environmentalism of the last decade, the differences with earlier expressions of concern should not be over-drawn. The new environmentalism is rooted in a reaction not only against the impact of technology on the built and natural environment, but against broader features of industrialism. This has always been an element in what Buttel (1980) distinguishes as the 'progressive' conservation movement. The ways in which industrialization generates discontents will be explored more fully in Chapter 4. But a brief discussion now will help in the understanding of the emergence of the new environmentalism in the late 1960s.

In all industrializing societies, the end of the nineteenth century saw reactions shaped by specific historical circumstances and national institutions to the growing impact of industrialization. The National Trust, for example, founded in Britain in 1895, was part of a general movement for the protection of open spaces and buildings of historic interest and natural beauty for public enjoyment. It was the precursor of the town planning movement and the foundation of the Town and Country Planning Association (1899), which sought to secure a public interest in the exercise of property rights. These were important departures from the prevailing ideologies of private property rights (Lowe *et al.* 1980) and laid the foundations for the extension of government powers seeking in a variety of ways to safeguard or promote the public interest and to counter the operation of purely market forces.

Similarly, in America, the bulk of the nation's land had been sold off to private owners by the end of the nineteenth century. Aggressive industrial exploitation of forests and mineral resources resulted in massive ecological damage (Buttel 1980). Support for conservation came from those who sought to curb the worst abuses of private ownership and to institute more rational and efficient procedures through 'scientific management' and government intervention. The Sierra Club, founded in 1892, was especially concerned that the sale of the public domain plus the destruction of forests was threatening to destroy the few remaining recreational areas. It too sought government intervention to protect the remaining forest areas from economic exploitation. In short, the progressive conservationists shared with the new environmentalists a conviction that the public interest needed protection against unbridled economic and market forces.[11]

The new environmentalism of the 1960s drew much of its support from the young, and especially in the U.S.A. It emerged in the wake of the civil rights and anti-war movements, which swept the campuses of American universities. It provided an expression for the emerging radicalism of the period, the so-called counter-culture. This was profoundly anti-industrial, with its decisive rejection of the work ethic, its condemnation of consumerism and material values, and its questioning of the rationality of a society which harnessed science to what were seen as the inhuman atrocities of the Vietnam war, and the ecological damage wrought by insecticides and industrial waste. In England, the campus radicalism was relatively muted, and eco-activists less prominent, though the dumping of thousands of bottles outside the headquarters of Cadbury Schweppes in 1971 set the tone for a more activist and youthful Friends of the Earth.

THE ENVIRONMENT AND THE PUBLIC

If the goal of a movement is to bring about some desired social change, the extent to which it can win public support is an important measure of its success and potential impact. Not all agree that there has been a decline in support for environmental protection. Much depends on how it is defined. If it is taken to include those activities concerned to promote the enjoyment of the countryside, then both membership and public support has increased (Lowe *et al.* 1980). But this study is concerned with the movement dimension of environmentalism; that is, with support for more radical policies of social change. And here there is evidence of levelling off, and even decline in support, though the picture is by no means clear. In Britain, membership of the Conservation Society has declined somewhat in recent years, but Friends of the Earth has continued to grow. There is a similar picture in the U.S.A. of a general levelling off since the mid-1970s and in some cases, decline (Buttel 1980).

But we need to distinguish between membership of organizations and the level of public support for environmental protection. And here, the picture is complex. Much depends on what is measured and how (Van Liere and Dunlap 1980). Dunlap and Dillman (1976) used a panel study method, interviewing the same subjects in Washington State in 1970 and 1974. Previous studies have focused on public perception of environmental degradation as a problem. Their approach was to ask whether members of the public were in favour of spending more or less money on a range of issues. They concluded that their data indicated a substantial decline in public support for protection, especially pollution, by comparison with other programmes, especially welfare. A further study in 1976 came to a similar conclusion (Dunlap *et al.* 1976, 1979). On the other hand, 82% of Washingtonians agree 'much progress has been made in cleaning up the environment during the last few years.' It is possible, therefore, that declining support measures satisfaction with progress rather than a decrease in the importance attached to environmental quality.

The extent of any decline in public concern about environmental issues since the high point of the early 1970s is not, therefore entirely clear. It depends in part how concern is defined and measured. Decline or no, there is evidence from a number of countries that the level of public concern and interest remains high. In the U.S.A., a survey conducted in July 1978 showed that around 30% considered air and water pollution and energy shortages as very serious, and another 46% as serious. Environmental problems were rated as considerably more serious than unemployment, though less serious than inflation. Moreover, 42% were prepared to pay higher prices to protect the enviroment, 52% thought the government was spending too little on the environment, and 53% believed that pollution control standards must continue to be improved, regardless of cost (Mitchell 1978). Such evidence certainly adds up to a picture of continuing concern for environmental protection.

In order to explore the nature and extent of support for enviromental issues in Britain, we have conducted a survey by postal questionnaire[12] of a number of different 'target' groups whom we believed would be likely to hold widely divergent views (see Appendix). The survey was in two phases. The first phase focused on groups within Britain. We were then approached by the Institute for Environment and Society, Berlin, to collaborate in an international survey which would provide a wider range of comparative data.[13] In reporting our findings, we will draw on the international data (from Germany, U.S.A. and Australia) where this points to important national differences.

In Britain, Friends of the Earth and the Conservation society are both examples of the new wave of radical environmentalists: in the USA, Environmental Action and Environmental Defense Fund provide examples of this kind, with the long established Sierra Club shifting to a more radical position. For the British survey of the 'new' environmentalists, we drew a sample from membership of the Conservation Society and Friends of the earth.[14] To provide comparisons with the new environmentalists, we sent questionnaires to members of the World Wildlife Fund, and for the international survey, to the Somerset Trust for Nature Conservation. To tap the views of a section of society whom we anticipated would contrast most sharply with environmentalists, we selected a sample of industrialists from the pages of the *Business Who's Who* and *Who's Who of British Engineers*, and a sample of trade union officials from the *Trade Union Handbook*. The international survey also included a sample of public officials. Finally, we included a sample of the 'general public', drawn from electoral registers.

Our first question was designed to tap perceptions of the seriousness of environmental problems: 'There's been a lot of talk about dangers facing society from pollution, population growth, and shortages of various kinds. How serious do you think such problems are?' Those who replied that they were extremely serious we classified as Catastrophists. Those who thought our problems were only moderately, not very, or not at all, serious, we categorized as Cornucopians. Over 40% of the two 'new' environmentalist associations sampled were by this definition Catastrophists, while the industrial sample were over-whelmingly Cornucopians (Table 1.2). While there are marked

Table 1.2. Seriousness of environmental problems

		Environ-mentalists %	Nature conserva-tionists %	Indust-rialists %	Trade union officials %	Public %
Catas-trophists	Extremely serious	41.8	39.0	6.6	19.3	19.3
Inter-mediate	Very serious	50.6	45.1	39.3	47.3	38.0
Cornu-copians	Moderately/not very/not at all serious	7.6	15.9	54.1	33.5	42.7
		100.0	100.0	100.0	100.0	100.0
	$n =$	(395)	(277)	(196)	(275)	(553)

differences between the target groups, 57% of the public believe environmental problems to be extremely or very serious. And 39% of the predominantly cornucopian industrialists believe the problems to be very serious. So by this criterion, there is a high level of awareness of environmental issues.

To explore perceptions of environmental dangers more fully, we asked respondents to indicate their agreement or disagreement with statements such as 'pollution is rising to dangerous levels' (see Appendix for full scale). The items in the scale cluster into three main groups. Firstly, there were those listing awareness of environmental damage, such as 'rivers and waterways are seriously threatened with pollution'; secondly, those indicating perception of shortages, such as 'there are likely to be serious and disruptive shortages of essential raw materials if things go on as they are'; and thirdly, there were statements about the destruction of natural habitats, such as 'some animals and plants are being threatened with extinction' (Table 1.3 Scales 1–3).

Table 1.3. Perceptions of environmental dangers

Scales	Environ- mentalists %	Nature conserva- tionists %	Indust- rialists %	Trade union officials %	Public %
1. Environmental damage					
Low	2.8	5.5	42.2	18.5	11.0
Medium	46.9	51.9	49.5	61.2	52.9
High	50.2	42.7	8.3	20.3	36.1
n	426	293	218	281	518
2. Environmental shortages					
Low	3.2	10.1	28.0	12.8	20.8
Medium	39.8	57.1	53.7	50.2	49.6
High	56.9	32.8	18.3	37.0	29.6
n	432	296	218	281	530
3. Nature protection					
Low	0.0	0.7	11.9	3.9	3.8
Medium	9.4	9.2	48.2	42.6	30.4
High	90.6	90.2	39.9	53.5	65.8
n	438	295	218	284	520

Three conclusions emerge. Firstly, there is a widespread recognition of threats to the environment, especially on scale 3—threats to some aspect of nature. Secondly, there are differences between groups. Most notable is the relatively low score of the industrial sample on all scales. The polarization is especially marked on the scale measuring environmental damage from causes such as pollution. Thirdly, on threats to nature and environmental damage, nature conservationists are close to the new environmentalists. But on shortages, their scores are closer to the public and to trade union officials.

In the international survey, we introduced additional questions to measure support for environmental action and policies. We also added public officials to our list of target groups. Respondents were asked to rank the urgency of a series of environmental issues (Table 1.4). Most groups rated a range of problems as very urgent (six or seven on a seven-point scale). What is

Table 1.4. Urgency of environmental issues

Very urgent — scale scores 6 & 7	Environ-mentalists %	Nature conserva-tionists %	Indust-rialists %	Public officials %	Trade union officials %	Public %
Noise	42.2	48.7	30.7	38.7	54.1	39.2
Air pollution	62.8	59.8	26.4	33.6	66.1	67.0
Water pollution	66.1	74.3	51.4	41.6	69.7	75.7
Overpopulation	65.9	45.8	38.1	29.0	33.5	52.9
Solid waste disposal	55.5	59.3	40.3	21.5	47.1	50.2
Toxic waste disposal	75.2	76.4	59.0	50.0	82.7	80.5
Nuclear waste	84.3	77.7	58.2	43.6	82.8	81.1
Townscape	82.2	79.4	53.3	54.0	65.3	67.2
Depletion of natural resources	90.3	93.3	65.2	62.5	77.1	80.7
Energy	87.3	74.8	73.0	57.9	74.3	78.1

Table 1.5. Support for raising taxes for pollution control

	Environ-mentalists %	Nature conserva-tionists %	Indust-rialists %	Public officials %	Trade union officials %	Public %
Strongly support (7–6)	85.4	63.5	29.2	42.0	52.9	35.0
Support (5)	8.1	24.5	33.8	36.0	23.4	28.5
Neutral (4)	5.2	9.0	25.4	14.0	13.3	17.8
Oppose (3)	0.6	1.0	6.5	4.3	4.5	7.3
Strongly oppose (2–1)	0.6	2.0	5.0	3.7	5.9	11.5
	100.0	100.0	100.0	100.0	100.0	100.0
n	(172)	(200)	(260)	(186)	(308)	(715)

especially remarkable is the high scores of the trade union officials. Indeed, on a number of issues such as noise, air pollution, toxic waste disposal, they ranked the issue as more urgent than did the environmentalists. The second notable conclusion is the consistently low rating of the officials in public office, whose scores were lower even than industrialists on most issues.

Realistic support for environmental policies involves willingness to pay. We asked respondents whether they would favour or oppose raising taxes to control pollution. Strongest support came from environmentalists and nature conversationists, and least from industrialists (Table 1.5). Again, trade union officials came fairly close to nature conservationists in their support. But there are other kinds of costs. Much has been made of the threat to employment resulting from environmental protection, especially in the U.S.A. We therefore faced respondents with the choice between protecting the environment and protecting jobs. Whereas trade union officials are more willing than industrialists to raise taxes, they are less willing to sacrifice jobs (Table 1.6). Only the environmentalists and nature conservationists have a

Table 1.6. Jobs versus the environment

Scale scores	Environ-mentalists %	Nature conserva-tionists %	Indust-rialists %	Public officials %	Trade union officials %	Public %
Protect jobs (1–2)	1.8	3.0	14.9	15.3	26.1	18.2
(3)	3.5	9.1	18.4	15.9	16.3	13.8
(4)	19.4	19.7	30.2	25.3	30.7	26.1
(5)	15.3	31.3	24.3	26.9	12.7	19.5
Protect environment (6–7)	60.0	36.9	16.2	16.4	14.0	22.3
	100.0	100.0	100.0	100.0	100.0	100.0
n	(170)	(198)	(255)	(182)	(306)	(717)

Table 1.7. Relative importance of objectives for government action

Rank order	Environ-mentalists	Nature conserva-tionists	Indust-rialists	Public officials	Trade union officials	Public
Welfare	4	4	4	4	2	2
Law and order	5	2	2	2	3	3
Economy	2	1	1	1	1	1
Energy	1	3	3	5	4	4
Environment	3	5	6	6	5	5
Foreign affairs	6	6	5	2	6	6

clear preference for protecting the environment. Finally, we tried to get some measure of the relative importance of environmental issues in relation to competing policy objectives. What is interesting here is the low ranking of the environment and the high priority given to the economy (Table 1.7).

The overall picture then is that the environment continues to be an important area of public concern.[15] There is a high level of awareness of the environmental dangers of various kinds, and a number of issues are judged to be urgent. The majority of the public would support raising taxes for pollution control, though there is a balance of opinion in favour of protecting jobs rather than the environment. But surveys of 'public opinion' aggregate the quite different views of politically significant groupings within society. When we disaggregate the public, and look at the positions of distinct publics within society, what emerges is the marked polarization both in perceptions of the environment and in the importance attached to environmental problems. What is especially notable is the way in which the beliefs and values of industrialists and public officials diverge, not only from those of enviromentalists, but also from the views of trade union officials. The exploration of the sources and significance of such differences is the main focus of this study.

IS ENVIRONMENTALISM ELITIST?

It has been widely argued that support for environmental concerns is elitist: that it is located mainly in the relatively better-off sections of society (Enzensberger 1974). But empirical studies do not support this simple assertion. It depends, of course, on what is being measured. We need to distinguish between awareness of environmental problems, and realistic support for environmental reform, such as willingness to pay more taxes. Moreover, it depends on the issue. We found different explanations for awareness of shortages compared with environmental damage (Appendix). Very extensive researches, mainly in the U.S.A., have had only limited success in locating the social bases of support for various measures of concern (Van Liere and Dunlap 1980).[16] Correlations between indices of concern and variables such as income, occupation, and party are low. Somewhat higher, but still modest, magnitudes are found for age, education, residence and political ideology. Certainly, the conventional measures of class (income, education and occupational status) have little explanatory value. They conclude that the 'limited utility of demographic variables in explaining variation in environmental concern points to the widespread distribution of concern in our society.'[17]

What does emerge, however, from both our own[18] and American studies is that the main clue is to be found not in demographic variables but in various measures of social and political beliefs and values. There are significant correlations between support for environmental reform and a cluster of political and social beliefs which can be most simply labelled as 'economic individualism'.[19] This is a finding of central importance to which we return in later chapters.

When we focus on sources of support for activist environmental pressure

Table 1.8. Occupations of environmentalists and public

	Environ-mentalists %	Public %
Commerce and industry		
professional and supervisory	14.3	13.6
clerical	5.6	12.2
Self-employed	9.6	4.8
Service, welfare, creative	38.4	12.2
Manual	5.4	28.2
Retired	9.1	7.8
Housewife	8.0	18.0
Unemployed	1.6	1.7
Student	8.0	1.4
	100.0	99.9
	$N = (427)$	$N = (294)$

Table 1.9. Characteristics of environmentalists compared

		Environ-mentalists	Nature conserva-tionists	Indust-rialists	Public officials	Public
		%	%	%	%	%
Age (years)	<20	5.0	0.3	0.0	0.0	8.4
	21–30	28.2	11.6	0.0	2.8	20.8
	31–40	24.8	18.4	2.8	17.0	19.4
	>40	41.9	69.7	97.2	80.2	51.4
	n	(439)	(310)	(217)	(283)	(558)
Education (years of education)	<10	0.0	n.m.	0.0	n.m.	38.2
	11–14	37.6	n.m.	31.0	n.m.	33.7
	>14	62.4	n.m.	69.0	n.m.	28.1
	n	(441)	n.m.	(216)	n.m.	(89)[+]
Market	M	35.6	53.2	76.4	82.9	58.3
	NM	64.4	46.8	23.6	17.1	41.7
	n	(368)	(216)	(212)	(263)	(441)
Income	<2000	17.2	12.1	n.m.	1.1	28.0
	2001–4000	32.4	29.7	n.m.	9.2	44.3
	4001–6000	23.8	25.8	n.m.	41.2	20.9
	6001–8000	15.4	12.9	n.m.	30.9	5.5
	>8000	11.3	19.5	n.m.	17.6	1.4
	n	(408)	(256)	n.m.	(272)	(422)
Politics	Left	18.4	0.7	1.5	26.2	9.4
	Mildly L	36.6	8.9	7.7	44.2	21.1
	Centre	23.9	25.6	17.9	18.5	33.7
	Mildly R	16.4	37.4	50.3	8.5	21.7
	Right	4.6	27.4	22.6	2.7	14.0
	n	(347)*	(270)	(195)	(260)	(360)*
Economic individualism	High	10.9	50.7	73.1	17.6	38.2
	Medium	55.8	44.8	25.5	55.1	57.1
	Low	33.3	5.0	1.4	27.3	4.8
	n	(414)	(280)	(212)	(267)	(482)

*Excluding 'no position on this spectrum'
[+] Bath only sampled
n.m. no measurement

groups, a different and clearer picture emerges.[20] Membership of the radical environmental associations we studied is heavily skewed towards a specific cluster of occupations. A high proportion are employed in the personal service professions and creative arts — as teachers, social workers, lecturers, doctors (Table 1.8). That is to say, they are employed in occupations outside the market sector, where goods and services are sold.

To say that environmentalists are middle class is true, but misleading. Industrialists too are well educated, and in the upper income bracket.[21] By any definition they too are middle class. Yet they are opposed to the environmentalist movement. Two crucial distinctions between environmental activists and other publics stand out. Firstly, the relation of environmentalists to the market place, and secondly, the differences in their political beliefs and values[22] (Table 1.9). In short, as it will be argued in more detail in Chapter 5, environmentalists can be identified as a specific fraction of the middle class.[23]

The data also lend ample support to our insistence on the need to distinguish between the new radical environmentalist movement and the older 'nature conservationist' associations. The crucial difference is in their political ideologies. The latter are markedly more right wing, and come close to the industrialists in their support for economic individualism. The significance of the differences will become clearer as we explore the beliefs and attitudes of radical environmentalists more fully in the next chapter.

NUCLEAR POWER AND THE ENVIRONMENT

During the last decade the centrality of different issues has changed. In the late 1960s, the main causes for concern were population and pollution. A decade later, the emphasis has shifted somewhat. Population, though still of top priority for some, has declined in importance, partly in response to the fall in birth rates in the advanced industrial societies. On the other hand, opposition to nuclear power has for many environmentalists become the key issue. The precise relationship between the environmentalist movement and the anti-nuclear movement is complex (Touraine 1979; Nelkin and Pollak 1980b). The two movements certainly draw on the same constituencies (Taylor and Pritchard 1980). But although they overlap, they are not identical. Much of the early opposition to nuclear power was related to particular sites (Surrey and Huggett 1976). Where, for example, a proposed site has threatened agricultural interests, including vineyards, this has generated powerful opposition from local farmers. The announcement of an expanded programme of nuclear installations following the oil crisis led to a more widespread movement with links formed between groups opposing individual sites. As opposition developed and became politicized, the debate broadened to include growing concern with technical issues related to specific nuclear hazards, and broader political, economic and social concerns (Del Sesto 1980), including the risks from terrorism, and the threat of nuclear power to individual freedom from the need for rigorous security procedures (Flood and Grove-White 1976). Opposition has come too from those who are opposed to what they see as the growing threats to the individual from centralized, bureaucratic decision making. In Europe citizen initiative groups have played a prominent part in opposition to environmental and nuclear issues. Environmentalists have certainly been strongly opposed to some aspects of the nuclear power programme. Friends of the Earth, in Britain, for example, have mounted a vigorous campaign, not only against the proposals for a reprocessing plant at Windscale, but also against any expansion of the nuclear programme.

Table 1.10. Attitudes to nuclear power

Agree — Scale score 5-7	Environ- mentalists %	Nature conserva- tionists %	Indust- rialists %	Public officials %	Trade union officials %	Public %
Nuclear wastes too dangerous	74.7	59.0	24.5	24.8	57.2	65.9
Nuclear accident increasingly likely	86.8	75.6	55.8	54.6	73.3	73.6
Need for nuclear power	32.0	34.3	77.0	62.2	64.6	42.5

This connection between environmentalism and opposition to nuclear power is confirmed by our survey data. The majority of both members of the Conservation Society and of the nature conservation sample agreed that nuclear waste is too dangerous and an accident increasingly likely (Table 1.10). Only a minority agreed on the need for nuclear power. Again, it is the industrialists and trade union officials who are most favourable. The trade unionists are closer to environmentalists on the dangers, but agree with industrialists on the need. (We will notice this ambivalence of trade union officials on other issues in subsequent chapters.)

The anti-nuclear movement appears, then, to overlap considerably with the environmentalist movement. As we will show in more detail later, the new environmentalists are similar to the C.N.D. marchers (Parkin 1968). But opposition to specific proposals as distinct from the more general opposition to nuclear power triggers coalitions of diverse interests. This includes environmentalists, as well as farmers and local residents, for whom the proposals offer a variety of threats.

ENVIRONMENTALISM, POLITICS AND THE FUTURE

Protesters on environmental issues have disrupted motorway inquiries, halted the construction of dams, the commissioning of nuclear generating stations, and delayed the opening of airports. In some countries, green or ecology parties have emerged in recent years, constituting a challenge which traditional parties could not ignore. And nuclear power shows every indication of becoming an issue for the mobilization of major protest and dissent. Moreover, if the pessimists are right, the disruptive effects of the exhaustion of many key fossil materials have yet to be felt. Indeed, in the field of energy, there has already been a dramatic change in the terms of the debate which is only partly due to the political factors which have reduced supplies and raised prices.[24] Moreover, left, centre, and right each has its own diagnosis of environmental ills and prescriptions for cure. Perceptions of the environment are inextricably tied up with political ideologies. As we have seen, the Marxist left traces problems of pollution and energy to the capitalist mode of production: the solution demands fundamental changes in the structure of society. The radical centre seeks a fundamental change in values and behaviour, either through the adoption of new individual life styles, or through social policies designed to trim economic activity to the carrying capacity of the earth. The right is pessimistic about democratic consensual change: coercion may be the only way to save the future (Stretton 1976).

The coherence and effectiveness of the movement and the translation of its ideals into plausible political programmes for action would certainly seem to present considerable difficulties. The paths of protesters may converge on the picket lines outside a nuclear site. But how far the groups with a common interest in protest can agree to march forward to common social goals is another question. It remains then to be discovered which of the repertoire of ideas resonates with the membership, and indeed stimulates a sympathetic response with wider constituencies. It is significant that the new environmentalism emerged at a point of crisis in recent history. The mid-1960s onwards saw a convulsive wave run through all advanced industrial societies, challenging the complacent optimism of the affluent society. Civil rights movements, movements for the liberation of females and homosexuals, citizen initiative groups, student unrest, and a rising tide of direct action, constitute the social background to the growth of the new environmentalism.

Can a study of the new environmentalism then throw light on these wider problems of social change? Was the 1960s possibly a turning point in the history of industrial societies? Is the rise of environmentalism indicative of more deep-seated changes in the values and aspirations of citizens which could have profound implications for the future of liberal democracies? These are the questions which future chapters will try to answer. But first we need to explore the basic question: how can we account for the polarization of views about an environmental crisis and about the future of industrial societies? Why do some believe society to be rushing headlong to catastrophe and disaster, while others look forward with confidence to a future world of plenty, a cornucopia overflowing with material wealth and leisure, in which automation and robots will take over the drudgery of work, and science and technology will have solved at least many of the problems which threaten human health and happiness? Why are there such widely differing perceptions of the nature and extent of environmental dangers, and of the sources of pollution and danger?

NOTES

1. 82% of Environmental Action members categorize themselves as liberal/radical, compared with 23% of members of the National Wildlife Federation (Mitchell 1980). Of course, many members of Friends of the Earth may well support the policies of older nature conservation societies by joining, for example, the National Trust. But the reverse is not true.
2. There is a vast and complex literature. For a more detailed analysis of the key texts and ideas see O'Riordan, 1976, Chapters 1-3, and Allaby 1971.

3. Some of the criticisms of this world model have been met by subsequent publications of the Club of Rome. A recent volume, for example, replaced the global world model with a much more refined model attempting regional projections and responding to regional differences (Mesarovic and Pestel 1975).

4. A similar objection argues that although quite substantial changes in any one parameter do not prevent predicted catastrophe

'much smaller changes in a number of parameters if applied simultaneously do indeed avert disaster. Now these combined changes are in the nature of purposeful adaptive processes which continuously occur in the real world through political, social, economic and technological actions. Forrester and Meadows characteristically ignored testing their model in this fashion.' (Jahoda 1973).

For a recent and powerful statement on limits see Catton, 1980.

5. This picture of the traditional community comes close to Tonnies' (1955) notion of the *Gemeinschaft* society:

'Insofar as enjoyment and labour are differentiated according to the very nature and capabilities of individuals, especially in such a manner that one part is entitled to guidance, the other is bound to obedience, this constitutes a natural law as an order of group life, which assigns a sphere and function, incorporating duties and privileges, to every will.'

6. Reductionism seeks to discover the properties of wholes by analysing the parts of which they are made up: whether it is atoms and fundamental particles, or the macro-molecules of the DNA code. See Chapter 4 for a more detailed discussion.

7. J. Passmore (1974) comments on the views of F. Fraser Darling —

'his simultaneous appeal to immanence and aristocracy . . . is only too typical, in its intellectual incoherence, of the Western mystical tradition. And the aristocrat who is also a servant — whether of God, of the people, or of the planet — is just as characteristic of authoritarianism' (p.11).

8. Mitchell (1980) makes a somewhat similar distinction between the 'soft', 'left' and 'deep' elements within the movement. 'Deep' ecology involves a rejection of economic growth, and the acceptance of an ecological perspective on society.

9. One other major theory of the rise and fall of social movements is the so-called 'natural history' theory, that all movements go through a natural progression, the decline attributable largely to boredom with the problem and awareness of the costs involved (Downs 1972). Evidence for the 'ecological backlash' and natural history theories is explored more fully in Dunlap and Van Liere 1977a.

10. This section draws heavily on Dunlap 1976 and Buttel 1980.

11. For a more detailed analysis of the evolution of the environmentalist movement in the U.S.A., see Andrews 1980.

12. For a more detailed statement of the research survey, its methodology and results, see Appendix.

13. This phase was assisted by a grant of DM10 000 from the Wissenschaftzentrum, Berlin.

14. We are grateful to Tom Burke and Dr. John Davoll for their help and encouragement. Any conclusions of course remain our, and do not necessarily reflect those of the associations sampled.

15. For comparative data on the U.S.A. and Germany, see Fietkau 1977, Milbrath 1975 and Mitchell 1978.

16. The literature is extensive. Van Liere and Dunlap 1980 reviewed some 20 empirical studies which explored bivariate relationships between various indices of concern and a number of demographic variables.

17. Buttel and Flinn 1978 arrive at a similar conclusion.

18. We subjected the data to multiple regression and path analysis. A full account is given in the Appendix.

19. This is explored more fully in Chapter 2.
20. Buttel and Flinn 1978 also argue for the need to differentiate between mass environmental concern and membership of organizations.
21. Although we did not ask our industrial sample to indicate income, the source of the sample supports the assertion that they are at least as well-off as the environmentalists.
22. Our findings confirm the conclusions of Van Liere and Dunlap (1980) that we need to turn from demographic to cognitive factors for explanations of support.
23. There are considerable methodological difficulties in identifying the factors which lead along the pathway to becoming an environmentalist (see Appendix). Take, for example, our observation that environmentalists are skewed towards non-market occupations. This does *not* mean that those in non-market occupations are significantly more likely to be environmentalists. We explore this more fully in Chapter 3.
24. The *Blueprint* predicted that demand for oil would exceed supply by the year 2000. At the time few accepted such gloomy predictions. What is interesting is the change in the climate of world opinion in the last seven years. True, the Six Days War and subsequent OPEC policies have all helped to undermine confidence. But what is especially interesting is the change in outlook of the oil companies themselves. The *Blueprint* was countered by the argument that reserves are much greater than they admit: that the rate of discovery is governed by the need to ensure supplies for the next 15 years, and that is why discovered reserves are no larger. But by 1979, Dr. Pearce, Chairman of Esso, in a paper to the Conference on Future Energy Concepts, presented data to show that on the most optimistic forecasts for oil supply, demand would exceed supply well before the year 2000. We return to this issue in Chapter 6.

CHAPTER 2

Environments at Risk

MAN AND NATURE

The way in which nature is seen differs widely between different cultures and between historical epochs (Williams 1972). In some cultures nature is benign, and man's relations with nature are harmonious and cooperative. At other times and in other places, nature is perceived as hostile, to be battled against, fought with, and overcome (Kluckhohn and Strodtbeck 1961). The natural environment is more than simply an objective fact: it is experienced, and given a subjectve meaning. The significance of rain in desert regions is not the same as in wet regions. A sunset to a sailor has overtones of meaning which are not experienced by the city dweller. Indeed, precisely the same climate may be experienced quite differently by neighbouring societies (Douglas 1972). So it is not just the facts of pollution, or the reduction in known reserves of non-renewable resources, or the threat to a rare species to which we must attend.[1] We need also to discover the underlying systems of beliefs and values which provide the framework for interpreting the evidence. We need to discover and bring to light the implicit cultural meanings which give significance to some explicit condition of nature.

Pollution is a good example. Pollution is a condition which departs from some standard of purity. Whether it is x parts per million, or $10x$ parts per million, the judgement that this particular level constitutes pollution goes beyond the readings on the dial to some judgement of purity and pollution. Pollution is then a social concept, not a scientific one. As Mary Douglas (1966) succinctly puts it, 'Dirt is matter out of place.' Beyond any differences there may be about the readings on the dials, there is always the question of meaning.

PARADIGMS AND PERCEPTIONS

So our problem is, can we discover the cultural contexts, the implicit meanings, which can explain the different ways in which Catastrophists and

Cornucopians see their environments and behave towards them? Our point of departure is the observation that the new radical environmentalists are at odds with industrial society. It is constantly and forcefully argued in the environmentalist literature that the roots of the ecological crisis are to be found in the values of modern industrial society with its commitment to growth and the domination of nature. Some go further and argue that the activities of industrial man are having a serious effect on social stability. Evidence is presented for the disintegration of industrial society, including such pathological manifestations as crime, delinquency, drug addiction, alcoholism, mental diseases, suicide — all of which, it is argued, are increasing exponentially in our major cities. It is clear from the writings of the environmentalists that there is a strongly negative evaluation of many of the central features of industrial society. They single out for special mention the size and scale of living — giant cities, and conurbations, and large-scale impersonal organizations, the highly centralized processes of decision-making, and the lack of individual participation and involvement in decisions which affect the life of the individual. It is these, they argue, which have contributed to the breakdown of any sense of community and belonging. Industrial society they see as an impersonal mass society, in which the individual is alienated and in which the deeper human values are denied. In short, modern man has paid too high a price for his Faustian bargain. In exchange for the power over his material environment and the wealth which technology has generated, he has lost his soul.

We want to argue then that the clue to the quite different ways in which environmentalists and industrialists — Catastrophists and Cornucopians — see their environments is to be found in contrasting patterns of beliefs and values. It is these which explain why the meaning and significance of some environmental issue, such as discharges of effluent into a river or shortages of fossil fuels, are so different. To carry the analysis further, we need to introduce the concept of paradigm. The term has acquired a particular significance in recent years through the work of Thomas Kuhn (1970). Kuhn was struck by the fact that science does not progress by a series of incremental discoveries, each building on the next. Periodically, some aspect of science undergoes a revolutionary change. Subsequent scientists 'see' some area of scientific phenomena differently. 'Facts' take on a different significance and meaning. Examples are the combustion theory of oxygen which displaced phlogiston theory, and the plate theory of continental drift. Paradigms then provide maps of what the world is believed to be like. They constitute guidelines for getting about and for identifying and solving problems. Above all, paradigms provide the framework of meaning within which 'facts' and experiences acquire significance and can be interpreted. But they have a normative as well as a cognitive dimension, indicating not only what is but what ought to be done. Now this is precisely what we have identified in our comparisons between industrialists and environmentalists. For reasons which will become clearer as we go along, we will label the industrialists' view the dominant social paradigm.[2] It is dominant not in the statistical sense of being held by most people, but in the sense that it is the paradigm held by dominant groups in industrial societies, and in the sense that it serves to legitimate and justify the institutions and practices of a market economy. As we will demonstrate in Chapter 5, it is the taken-for-granted common-sensical view which usually determines the outcome of debates on environmental issues.

A systematic and schematic outline of the dominant and contrasting environmentalist paradigms is given in Table 2.1.[3] The first and most

Table 2.1. Counter paradigms

	Dominant Paradigm	Alternative Environmental Paradigm
Core values	Material (economic growth)	Non-material (self-actualization)
	Natural environment valued as resource	Natural environment intrinsically valued
	Domination over nature	Harmony with nature
Economy	Market forces	Public interest
	Risk and reward	Safety
	Rewards for achievement	Incomes related to need
	Differentials	*Egalitarian
	Individual self-help	Collective/social provision
Polity	Authoritative structures: (experts influential)	Participative structures: (citizen/ worker involvement)
	Hierarchical	*Non-hierarchical
	Law and order	*Liberation
Society	Centralized	Decentralized
	Large-scale	Small-scale
	Associational	Communal
	Ordered	*Flexible
Nature	Ample reserves	Earth's resources limited
	Nature hostile/neutral	Nature benign
	Environment controllable	Nature delicately balanced
Knowledge	Confidence in science and technology	Limits to science
	Rationality of means	Rationality of ends
	Separation of fact/value, thought/feeling	Integration of fact/value, thought/feeling

*Some environmentalists want a return to small-scale communities because they provide a traditional organic order — differentiated, hierarchical, and stable.

important difference centres around the core values of the creation of material wealth. It is this, it can be argued, which is the master value of industrialism. In an attack on the environmentalists, C. C. Pocock (Managing Director of Shell International) made his priorities quite explicit:

'. . . we see a huge agricultural dam . . . halted by environmentalists when it was nearly finished, and then scrapped to protect some obscure fish. . . . It has been well said, "The creation of wealth in a world of want is a moral duty." I suggest that that morality is just as valid as the morality of the environmentalists.'

The creation of 'wealth'[4] for the industrialists is a moral imperative. And if wealth is the name of the game, then the rules for winning that game follow: rewards for enterprise and risk, a free market, and creating a climate in which individuals are motivated to look after themselves and not to turn to others. Production and distribution require organization and direction: the division of labour is only possible within the framework of centralized hierarchically structured and imperatively coordinated organizations. Respect for legitimate authority—both at the industrial and political level—provides the essential context of law and order within which the forces of production and the free market operate. The task of politics is to see that the game is played according to the rules but not to interfere with the players.

There is another subtle, but powerful thread running through the dominant social paradigm. Some have traced it to the influence of the Christian doctrine of man's lordship over the earth (Lynn White 1967). This is both a value-orientation and a belief: commitment to the goal of mastery and domination over nature, and the belief that man has both the right and the ability to use nature instrumentally for his own ends and purposes. There is not only a moral dimension to man's relations with nature but also an associated belief about man's ability to subjugate natural forces and processes to his own ends: a confidence in particular that science and technology can provide the means, and that given the resources and the knowledge, the possibilities in the long run are almost boundless. Belief in the powers of science, not only as a body of knowledge, but in 'the scientific method', has become an article of faith as fundamental to the business civilization as was religious faith to an earlier social order.

These then are the twin pillars of the enterprise culture: the moral imperative to 'wealth' production, and the associated moral conviction of the right to dominate nature and to harness the natural environment to this end. On this foundation there arises a set of rules based on beliefs about how society and nature work, from which flow prescriptions for action. The alternative environmental paradigm polarizes on almost every issue. The first and most obvious point of difference is the environmentalists' opposition to the dominant value attached to economic growth. This in turn is reinforced by beliefs that the earth's resources are finite—a view encapsulted in Boulding's telling metaphor 'spaceship earth'. But their disagreement with the central values and beliefs of the dominant social paradigm runs deeper than this. Not only do they challenge the importance attached to material and economic goals, they by contrast give much higher priority to the realization of non-material values—to social relationships and community, to the exercise of human skills and capacities, and to increased participation in decisions that affect our daily lives. They disagree too with the beliefs of the dominant social paradigm about the way society works. They have little confidence in science and technology to come up with a technological fix to solve the problems of material and energy shortages. And this is in part rooted in a different view of nature which stresses the delicate balance of ecological systems and possible irreversible damage which may result from the interventions of high technology. They question whether the market is the best way to supply people with the things they want, and the importance of differentials as rewards for skill and achievement. They hold a completely different world view, with different beliefs about the way society works, and about what should be the values and goals guiding policy and the criteria for choice. It is, in short, a counter-paradigm.

Table 2.2. Alternative beliefs and values

	Environ-mental-ists %	Nature conserva-tionists %	Indust-rialists %	Trades unionists %	Public %
1. Post-material Values					
Low	4.2	31.0	54.4	14.2	25.7
Medium	74.6	66.0	44.2	79.8	72.2
High	21.2	3.1	1.4	6.0	2.1
n	425	294	215	282	529
2. Anti-economic Individualism					
Low	10.9	50.7	73.1	17.6	38.2
Medium	55.8	44.3	25.5	55.1	57.1
High	33.3	5.0	1.4	27.3	4.8
n	414	280	212	267	482
3. Anti-industrialism					
Low	1.9	10.8	31.3	9.7	13.3
Medium	57.9	79.6	65.4	74.3	81.0
High	41.0	9.7	3.3	16.0	5.7
n	416	279	211	268	510
4. Anti-science					
Low	22.1	42.6	78.5	69.4	68.0
Medium	60.9	53.7	20.5	29.6	29.4
High	17.0	3.7	0.9	1.1	2.6
n	430	296	219	284	531

Our surveys of various publics enabled us to put this model to the test and to get some sort of measures of the varying degrees of support for or opposition to these two contrasting paradigms. To explore support for material values, we adopted a modified form of Inglehart's post-material values scale, which has been widely used in international studies. Environmentalists came out as 'post-materialists', attaching high priority to non-material goals such as giving people more say in impotant government decisions, and progressing towards a less impersonal, more humane society. By contrast, industrialists emerged strongly as 'materialists', giving priority to such goals as a strong defence force, fighting rising prices, and maintaining a stable economy (Table 2.2 scale 1).

In order to explore their social preferences and ideals more fully, we identified what seemed to us to be those aspects of society which environmentalists wished to encourage, based on a wide reading of environmentalist literature. But we also identified those issues which emerged from overt criticisms of environmentalists, particularly from industrialists and those sympathetic to their cause. On the basis of this analysis, we presented respondents with a series of alternatives and asked them which they would prefer in their ideal society (Appendix). In this way we hoped to tap social values realistically. Again, the differences are striking (Table 2.2 scale 2). Industrialists give strong support for a cluster of items that could loosely be labelled economic individualism: for economic growth, rewards for achievement, the operation of market forces, authority, law and order.[5] The environmentalists, by contrast, want a very different kind of society, in which much more emphasis is placed on satisfying work, participation in decisions, and in which the supremacy of the market is subjected to the public interest (Figures 2.1 and 2.2).

On a scale of measures to tap central features of industrial society, the differences were equally marked. A series of items was designed to tap

FACTOR A: WEALTH CREATION VS. LIMITS TO GROWTH

Item no.	*Factor Loading*
1. A society in which there is a continually growing economy, or one in which there is no growth?	0.612
2. A society in which production is selective (e.g. towards products which use little energy), or one which aims to satisfy the market for consumer goods?	-0.474
3. An economy geared to overcoming limits to growth (e.g. from exhaustion of some raw materials), or one which accepts that there are limits to growth?	0.703

FACTOR B: MARKET VS. NON-MARKET

5. A society with strong law and order, or one which attaches relatively less importance to law and order?	0.553
9. A society which emphasizes rewards for talent and achievement, or one where the emphasis is on other criteria (such as need)?	0.684
10. A predominantly capitalist society, in which market forces and private interests predominate or a predominantly socialist society, in which public interests and a controlled market predominate?	0.565
15. A society which recognizes differentials related to skill, education and achievement, or one which emphasizes similar incomes and rewards for everybody?	0.680

FACTOR C: AUTHORITY VS. PARTICIPATION

6. A society in which the individual has a considerable say in how things get decided at his work-place, or one in which decisions (after consultation) are left to management?	-0.588
7. A society which emphasizes work which is humanly satisfying, or one where work is controlled mainly by the needs of industry?	-0.427
13. A society which emphasizes the participation of individuals in major government decisions, or one which leaves the final decisions to the judgement of the elected government?	-0.690
14. A society which strengthens the influence of experts in complex government decisions (such as nuclear energy), or one which facilitates the participation of the 'man in the street'?	0.523

FACTOR D: INDIVIDUAL VS. COLLECTIVE

4. A society in which the individual lives his life within a community, or one in which the individual is free to go his own way?	-0.519
11. A society which emphasizes the social and collective provision of welfare or one where the individual is encouraged to look after himself?	-0.542
12. A society which has a strong emphasis on community and belonging, or one where the emphasis is on individualism?	-0.811

Figure 2.1. Factor analysis of social ideals

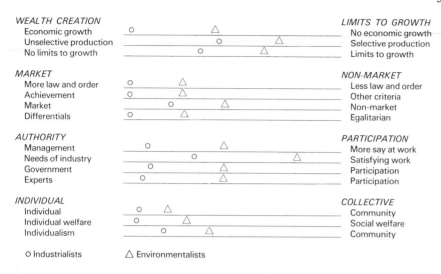

Figure 2.2. Social ideals of environmentalists and industrialists

attitudes towards industrial society, such as 'our present way of life is much too wasteful of resources', 'on balance the advantages of cities outweigh their disadvantages', 'vigorous industrial output is the mark of a health society', and 'there are forces at work in modern societies which stimulate a lot of artificial wants for things that we do not really need.' Environmentalists again stood out as having a high anti-industrial society score (Table 2.2 scale 3).

Although we did not include questions on relations with the natural environment, a survey in the U.S.A. has done so, with significant results (Dunlap and Van Liere 1978a). A sample of the general public and of an environmental organization were presented with a series of agree/disagree statements. The results, as expected, show very strong support among the environmentalists for what the researchers call the new environmental paradigm, for example: 'The balance of nature is very delicate and easily upset' (80% agree); 'Mankind was created to rule over the rest of nature' (53% disagree); 'Plants and animals exist primarily to be used by humans' (61% disagree); and 'Humans must live in harmony with nature in order to survive' (96% agree). A further 83% agree with the metaphor 'spaceship earth', and 75% that there are limits to growth. We do not, of course, know how industrialists and other sections of the public strongly committed to growth would respond. What we can conclude is that so far as the American public is concerned, there is widespread rejection of any moral justification for man's predatory relations with nature.

Finally, industrialists and environmentalists differ in their attitudes towards science and technology. Environmentalists and industrialists differed considerably in their view on such statements as 'science and technology provide man with his best hope for the future', 'the bad effects of technology outweigh its advantages', and 'science and technology can solve our problems by finding new sources of energy and materials, and ways of increasing food production' (Table 2.2 scale 4).

It is not, of course, being claimed that there are only two paradigms. Indeed, we will be particularly concerned in the final two chapters to explore areas of agreement and disagreement between other major groups in society with whom environmentalists may be able to form alliances and coalitions. There is clearly very much in common between the new environmentalists and trade union officials. This chapter deliberately focuses on the extremes. In this way we hope to achieve a sharper understanding of environmentaists by contrasting the movement with those whose views are diametrically opposed.

POLLUTION AND DANGER

So, to understand why environmentalists perceive more pollution, more environmental dangers, and are more pessimistic about the future, we have to see the world as they see it. And equally, to understand why industrialists perceive less pollution and danger, we need to switch to their paradigm. The world of the environmentalists is a very different world from that of the cornucopian industrialists. Each 'sees' their environment differently. The 'objective facts' about pollution and environmental damage and shortages do not and cannot exist in some king of cognitive and moral vacuum. Indeed, as we have already argued, the very notion of pollution involves a moral judgement: a threat to some standard of purity. Society (or some section of it) decides that the existence of a substance in an environment above a certain level constitutes a threat to some value. It is this which is defined as pollution. Rules against pollution then are always part of the defence of a specific social order. And this is at heart a moral order. This is where environmentalists and industrialists differ; they support different social and moral orders. It is this which may go far to explain why industrialists perceive less pollution and danger. The discharge of waste into rivers does not threaten their world of wealth creation: it is seen as less of a danger to their moral and social order. The level at which it becomes a danger, and therefore defined as *pollution*, is simply different.

At the nub of the debate, then, there is a conflict of values—the value placed on material versus non-material goals; traditional versus modern life styles. It is a debate about the nature of the good society. This is not the kind of thing that can easily be settled by appeal to facts and rational argument. An argument about values is not an easy argument to win. And here we can again seek inspiration from Mary Douglas's anthropological studies. What intrigues her are the ways in which different human societies see their environments, identify pollution, and single our polluters. 'Time, money, God and nature', she says, 'are the universal trump cards plunked down to win an argument' (Douglas 1972 p.134). So the 'laws of nature are dragged in to sanction the moral code: this kind of disease is caught by adultery, that by incest; this meteorological disaster is the effect of political disloyalty, that the effect of impiety' (Douglas 1966 p.13). In advanced industrial societies too, the environment has become a doom-point: a trump card thrown down by the Catastrophists to win a moral argument.

What the environmentalists are saying is that the society we have got is bad: that the way we behave is against 'Nature'; our children will suffer, and time is running out. They want a more convivial society in which community replaces unbridled individualism, in which people are valued as individuals and not for what they have achieved, in which work is humanly satisfying, and in which individuals have more say in the decisions which affect their lives. When environmentalists protest about pollution, they are not just arguing about the acidity of effluent, or the dangers of low level radiation. They are also saying that it is a bad society which treats its environment this way. It is a very different kind of society and a different relation between man and his environment which the industrialists are defending with equal moral fervour. They, by contrast, believe in a society dedicated to the production of wealth, in which individuals are set free from constraints and restrictions, and are rewarded for what they achieve; in which efficiency and the needs of industry are the touchstones of policy. If the environment takes a knock or two, then this is the price we pay for the pursuit of the greater good. So the way the environment is seen and optimism or pessimism for the future are all part and parcel of a general cosmology or world view, which includes values, conceptions of nature, of human nature, of theories of how we know and understand the world, and theories of how society works best. And we can understand why the environmentalists desperately need some trump cards to help them win a moral argument: though this should in no way detract from the intrinsic merits of their case. They are taking on extremely powerful forces in modern industrial societies. Indeed, they are challenging its core values.

IMPLICIT MEANINGS

This then is the clue to the character of the dialogue between environmentalists and their opponents. The debate on a whole spectrum of environmental issues abounds with charges of irrationality, sentiment and emotion — on both sides. Too often, the protaganists face each other in a spirit of exasperation, talking past each other with mutual incomprehension. It is a dialogue of the blind talking to the deaf. Nor can the debate be settled by appeals to facts. We need to grasp the implicit cultural meanings which underlie the dialogue.

This is the crucial significance of Kuhn's notion of paradigms: they generate major problems of communication and understanding. Indeed, Kuhn argued that opposing paradigms may be incommensurable, and defeat understanding. To adopt a new paradigm is frequently akin to a conversion experience. Once you have come to see the world from the new view point it is hard to switch and to imagine how you saw it before. It is analogous to the *Gestalt* switch which occurs when a diagram of a staircase suddenly 'flips' from top-down to bottom-up perspective. It took a decade or two to convince treasury officials not to look at government expenditure in the same way that a prudent individual runs his personal economy: that in hard times, governments should spend and not save. But once they had done so, it became orthodox economic policy: a switch from one economic paradigm to another had occurred. Industrialists and environmentalists, we suggest, inhabit different worlds.[6] From where they each stand, the world looks different. What is rational and reasonable from one perspective is irrational from another.[7] If the goal is maximizing economic output, then nuclear risks are not only justified but it would be unreasonable not to take them. From another perspective, from the viewpoint of a quite different set of beliefs about how the world works, and quite different aims for some kind of more convivial society, to take even the smallest risks for future generations stimulates a moral indignation which justifies unorthodox political action that crosses the threshold of legality. It is the taken-for-grantedness, the commonsensical character of each side's views which lies at the root of incomprehension. The implications of this for political debate are serious and worrying — an issue to which we return in Chapter 5.

ENVIRONMENT AND SOCIETY

Concern about environmental protection means different things to different groups in society. Nature can be protected for different reasons: aesthetic, scientific, economic, political. Or concern can spring from a desire to preserve amenities, or simply from the pleasure derived from enjoying wildlife and natural habitats. Such motives are widespread. Increasing affluence and leisure is associated with the growing enjoyment of outdoor life and activities, and the substantial rise in membership of environmental associations, defined in this very broad sense (Lowe *et al.*, 1980). It is not surprising then to find that members of conservationist and preservationist societies differ little from the general public, except in being better off, and in attaching particular importance to the protection of nature. And there is some justification in labelling them as being preoccupied with 'middle class' concerns and promoting middle class interests (Enzensberger 1974).

But, throughout, we have emphasized the distinction between the new radical environmentalism and the traditional nature conservation movement. Our data amply justify this distinction. The nature conservationists differ in their perception of environmental changes, only in being considerably less concerned with shortages. But they do not share with the radical environmentalists anti-industrial society attitudes, nor are they post-materialists. Above all, they support the dominant social paradigm. In short, they do not wish to change society, nor do they see the protection of the environment as necessitating any such changes.

The radical environmentalists are different. They want a different kind of society. And they use the environment as a lever to try to bring about the kind of changes they want. Trade unionists too want what is in many ways a similar kind of society, but they go about it by more direct political means. Environmentalists operate through pressure groups rather than party politics. Ecology or 'green' parties have won some support. But nowhere are they more than a marginal threat to established political alignments.

We will need to return to this whole question of the politics of the environment and explore the issues raised. But first there are a number of questions which remain unanswered about support for environmentalism. We have shown that environmentalists occupy particular locations in the social structure. They are younger, better educated, left in politics, and more likely to be employed in the non-market sector. What is the connection between their beliefs and attitudes and their social roles? Statistical analysis can establish the interconnection between variables. But we now need to try to *understand* the correlations. Why are the young more post-material and anti-industrial society? And why are environmentalists likely to be employed in non-market sector occupations? And are the changes which have led to the rise of radical environmentalism pointers to more deep-seated social changes? What is the meaning of the patterns uncovered by statistical analyses? It is to these questions that we now turn.

NOTES

1. It is not implied that there are no questions of 'fact', (though these are more problematic than is often realized), but only that 'objective' evidence is but one side of the equation. The world is always perceived and known by subjects who constitute the inescapable and residual subjective element in human knowledge.
2. For an early exploration of the idea of a new environmental paradigm see Pirages 1977.
3. Dunlap and Van Liere arrived at a very similar formulation by a comparable route. They too identified the dimensions of the dominant social paradigm by reviewing the literature which argued that the root of the ecological crisis is to be found in the basic values and beliefs of American society. After factor analysis their dimensions emerge as:
   (a) support for *laissez faire*—limited government regulation;
   (b) faith in material abundance;
   (c) faith in science and technology;
   (d) support for the *status quo*;
   (e) support for private property;
   (f) support for individual rights;
   (g) support for economic growth.
4. 'Wealth' is of course a euphemism for profit. It is the sale of goods and services in the market place which is central, regardless of the contribution these make to welfare. So the sale of medical services would be defined as wealth creation; their provision through a national health service would not.
5. Pilot studies enabled us to eliminate those items which did not discriminate. We subjected the remaining list to factor analysis, a statistical technique for discovering such patterns through tracing the interconnection between replies on individual items. The principal factor showed loadings on a series of items which clearly reflect the main elements in the dominant social paradigm.

6. This assumes adopting a broadly phenomenological position that it is perceptions and beliefs about reality which constitute knowledge, and as Thomas and Znaniecki long ago pointed out, it is what is believed to be real that determines actions.
7. In fact, there is plenty of emotion in the defence of the free enterprise system as well as in its opposition.

CHAPTER 3

World-views in Transition

So, environmentalists not only attach a different meaning to environmental dangers compared with industrialists, trade unionists and nature conservationists: they are also employed in particular kinds of jobs, differ in politics, are anti-science and technology, and are antagonistic towards industrial society. Why do they reject material values and the dominant ideology? What is it about their particular experiences in society which have led them to embrace such beliefs and values?

Now the problem is to explain how groups within society come to have such different views of the world. There are three main perspectives which may help. Firstly, there is the view that the culture of a group or society reflects social reality and social experiences. Durkheim (1912), for example, explored the ways in which categories of thought (time and space, or the distinction between the religious and the secular), are symbolic representations of the experiences of living in society. An alternative related version is Marx's view that most knowledge is heavily influenced by interests generated by positions occupied within the social structure, especially in relation to the means of production. According to this view, knowledge and beliefs are generally ideological in the sense that they function to obscure the real underlying interests.[1] The second major perspective pushed the process further back, and seeks an understanding of the determination of beliefs in the process of socialization. According to this view, the influence of family and upbringing exercises a powerful influence on, for example, the formation of political ideologies or religious beliefs. This approach explains only how different groups within society come to embrace any particular element of culture. It cannot explain the genesis of the beliefs themselves. Yet a third alternative is more flexible and less deterministic. It starts from the recognition that any but the simplest cultures are in fact very complex and provide a variety of alternative beliefs and values. According to this view, we have a whole gazetteer of maps to help us find our way through different parts of our social territory. So we thumb the pages to find guides to the bits we need. We can even make our own maps by piecing together bits which seem to offer the best fit. This is a more voluntaristic perspective, which seeks the clue to beliefs in the intentions and purposes which individuals embrace.[2] These approaches are sociological, in the sense that they all explore the relation between beliefs and the positions which individuals occupy in the social structure.

SITUATIONS AND VALUES

We may take as a starting point our observation that two-thirds of our sample of radical environmentalists were employed in the non-market sector. It is hardly surprising that our sample of industrialists should be pro-industrial society, support material values, science and technology, and favour economic individualism.[3] By the same argument, it is not surprising to find some kind of congruence or fit between the values and beliefs of environmentalists and their occupations. For the point is, that not all segments of society are dedicated to maximizing economic values. Despite the centrality of economic goals and institutions, non-market sub-systems such as the family, education and welfare are essential and indispensable elements within an industrial society. And their goals and values are not only different but even antagonistic to those of the sub-systems which operate within the market place. The goals of family life, the values that its members seek to maximize, the criteria for conduct are predominantly non-economic. Individuals are valued as persons rather than for what they have achieved; needs are met regardless of ability to pay. The unconditional commitments and loyalties of the family are far removed from the contractual relations of the market place. Affection and companionship are highly valued goals, and mutual sexual satisfaction is expected to take place within this context. Indeed, the exchange of sex for monetary payments is generally condemned: even in a society dominated by a market mentality, the commercialization of sex is only grudgingly admitted and strictly regulated. In the same way, the intrusion of the values of kinship into economic or political affairs is equally condemned. To offer political posts or contracts to relatives is nepotism and even corruption: only the criteria of competence relevant to the goal of the sub-system can be admitted. Market and non-market sub-systems not only pursue different values and goals, but have different criteria of success, offer different motivations and rewards and are differently structured and organized (Figure 3.1).

Of course, individuals do not have to internalize the values of the social situations in which they find themselves (Goffman 1969). And we are certainly not trying to paint a simple determinist picture. There is no doubt, for example, of the extremely high commitment of many scientists to the discovery of knowledge (Eiduson 1962). But this does not mean that they are indifferent to material values and rewards: only that these are lower in their scale of priorities. Insofar as they may also occupy roles in the market sector economic criteria are relevant for evaluating the economic rewards of the job.

It is this which could explain what Marsh (1977) considered to be an anomaly. He found that post-materialists tended to be more rather than less

	Market sub-systems	Non-market sub-systems
Goals/values	Material: production of goods and services for sale	Non-material: political, welfare, personal development
Criteria of performance	Economic: cost-effectiveness, efficiency	Non-economic: quality (of professional service)
Rewards, motives, incentives	Financial: instrumental involvement	Professional (e.g. recognition) expressive involvement self-actualization
Organizational context	Hierarchical: imperatively coordinated; legal–rational authority	Collegiate, participative, authority derived from personal qualities
Social relations	Associational/contractual, competitive (cash nexus)	Communal-cooperative (non-economic criteria)
Conditions for survival	Short-term — financial solvency: longer term — competitive position in market	Long-term — competent performance; qualitative criteria; social recognition
Rationality	Technical/instrumental	Value

Figure 3.1. Alternative social systems

critical of their material circumstances.[4] His solution was to develop a distinction between personal and public values: the former operating in the individual's private life. Goals which individuals seek to maximize for society may not correspond precisely to the hierarchy of values which operates in their personal lives. Perhaps environmentalists in market occupations are private materialists and public post-materialists.

The alternative explanation which we are suggesting here is that values are relevant to situations. We would not expect the most ardent materialist and supporter of economic individualism to allow such values and ideals to dominate family relationships and more intimate personal relations and loyalties. So when individuals are presented with a list of social goals, there is no necessary inconsistency if they emphasize goals for society which differ from those appropriate for areas of their personal lives. It is quite consistent to act according to material values in an occupation (to be dissatisfied with the salary, for example), and at the same time to give low priority to economic growth as a goal for society.

ENVIRONMENTS AND COSMOLOGIES

So, we can point to some kind of congruence or fit between values and contexts. Part of the explanation may be that different values are relevant in different situations. But it is also possible that values and world views are largely shaped by social contexts. Perhaps the very different perceptions of their social worlds held by environmentalists and industrialists simply reflects the realities of their everyday existences?

Again we can turn to the work of anthropologists for a convincing and persuasive explanation along these lines. We have already painted a picture of the world views of industrialists. What is fascinating about this image of the rugged individualism of the market place is that it is by no means confined to advanced industrial societies. Anthropologists describe other societies which look remarkably similar, and where some behave in ways which are indistinguishable. Can we then learn from wider studies why some are prepared to dice with danger, to play Russian roulette with their environments, and are relatively indifferent to pollution, while others seek to draw protective boundaries, to keep out pollution and polluters, and to bring collective sanctions against the risk-takers?

The 'Big Man' system, as it is called in New Guinea, serves as an example of a system which is found world-wide in tribal societies (Douglas 1970). 'The Big Man is a forceful, competitive entrepreneur who builds up a massive personal network through his many wives, his relatives, his followers and his students or henchmen' (Thompson 1978). He is at the centre of the network whose members he can manipulate. Now let us contrast this with those societies with a strong caste system, such as India or Nepal. Individual members have little personal freedom of action. Each occupies a position in a hierarchy in which behaviour is narrowly prescribed by rules. In western societies, the armed forces and civil service provide familiar examples.

If we look at these opposing social structures, we can detect two main dimensions which generate restrictions. Firstly, there are the pressures that derive from being caught up in a network of reciprocal group obligations. Secondly, there are the prescriptions which flow from institutionalized sets of rules and procedures. So, we have four possible social contexts, according to whether they are high or low on rules and prescriptions, and whether they are strongly or weakly bounded by group pressures.[5] These dimensions demarcate the social space within which individuals can move. And what is fascinating about this typology is its promise in helping us to understand risk-taking or - avoiding behaviour, and concern with purity and pollution. Each of these four social contexts, argues Mary Douglas, generates a particular cosmology. She suggests that culture is not infinitely variable, and that these two dimensions set limits to the 'range of cosmological possibilities they can land themselves with by choosing to deal with their social problems in one way rather than another' (Douglas 1970, p.7). These cosmologies provide a map of what the world is like, how it operates, and indicate what kinds of actions are possible and necessary (Figure 3.2).

The 'Big Men' form a familiar category. They are the manipulators. Status is achieved by individual effort, in marked contrast to the strict rules which prescribe status within the caste. Alliances are made according to their expected pay-off, free from obligations to kith, kin, tribe, or community. Access to the Big Man is therefore a taxing problem. The private bathroom, like the ex-directory telephone, protects him from intrusions where all other insulating barriers have gone down. Large-scale feasts are a way of maximizing the use of time in personal contacts. Indeed, time is of the essence.

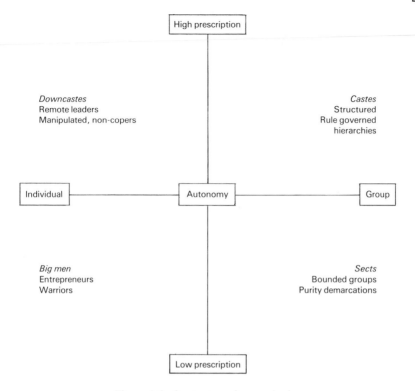

Figure 3.2. Contexts and cosmologies

Action is directed to quick gains and time perspectives are short. The environment is an external resource available for exploitation free of any constraints or prescriptions. Risk is a fact of life.

Moving up group and towards prescription, not only social relations but the environment changes. In caste society rules and prescriptions are everywhere. Monastic life, military societies and bureaucracies are good examples. Prescriptions govern in minute detail relations between persons and between man and nature. And a strong group ensures that the rules are collectively enforced. Anxiety about purity and pollution are taken care of by the highly institutionalized procedures which keep every individual and every thing in its ordained place. And just as society is seen to be highly structured, so too, nature is perceived as orderly and rule governed, and any transgression brings sanctions and punishment.

In the sects, by contrast, anxiety about purity and pollution is at its maximum. Here, there is low prescription, an absence of highly codified rules and procedures. A strong collectivity without hierarchy maximizes group control, and also generates uncertainties. There is particular anxiety about preserving group boundaries and who is in and who out. Groups are small: size is a threat to cohesion. The group watch anxiously for signs of defilement.

And the polluters are singled out for exclusion and expulsion. The absence of ritual and prescription leaves the environment especially vulnerable, to be saved only by the constant collective vigil. Unlike the castes where nature too is orderly, here nature is capricious and may easily get out of control.

The downcastes are at the bottom of the heap, unprotected by any collectivity or group, and at the mercy of imposed prescriptions. These are the 'rubbish men', manipulated by others, unable to confer value, forced to accept the valuations of others and to take what is left over (Thompson 1979a). Powerless in the face of forces over which they have no control, they can only relate fatalistically to their environment.

Each of these social structural situations then generates a picture of what the world is like, which sets limits to how to act and what can be done. But each has its penalties and inherent instabilities. The sects, for example, with their strong collectivity, have leadership problems. Essentially egalitarian, rules defining hierarchy and status would threaten communality. Leaders are charismatic figures whose authority flows from their special (magical) qualities. And experts too are out of place since they too threaten communality. Castes are highly stable, but also very restrictive. They provide a particularly secure environment, but at the cost of heavy restrictions. The Big Men are most at risk. Unwilling to limit their own freedom of action by constraints generated by collectivity or prescription, it is tempting for them to move towards prescriptions for others. Indeed, when things look like getting out of hand, they may seek to shelter beneath the protective cover of the ready-made caste systems like the family where status is ascribed and there are moral imperatives like loyalty and altruism. For the downcastes, they can choose either the consolations of fatalistic philosophies, or they can exchange their vulnerable individualism and prescriptive repression for the collective repression of the sect.

There is of course one fifth alternative: to seek to escape from the twin pressures of group and prescription into a haven of personal autonomy. This, perhaps, is the clue to the self-sufficiency movement. Here the search is for an environment which is not at the mercy of the whims, restrictions and repressions of the Big Men, the castes and the sects. The dream is for a stable environment which maximizes personal autonomy, and in which the individual is master of his own destiny and fate. It is a different kind of individualism from that of the Big Men—not the individualism of the buccaneer, dominating others, which generates its own insecurities—the fear of being toppled. It is a less stressful individualism, perhaps better described as the individuality of self-determination. It is in some ways misleading to think of it as the intersection of the two dimensions. We need a three-dimensional model,[6] which adds power to prescription and group. The marketeer operates not only in a social structure free from constraints, but he controls the system. He is free from prescriptions, but he imposes them on others. Upper caste dominates low caste. Sect leaders control followers. Autonomy is an escape from these three constraints.

So what can we now say about risk-taking and avoiding? Mary Douglas's theory is admittedly speculative and controversial. But so is all theory to the extent that it goes beyond mere description. Quite apart from the substantial anthropological evidence on which it rests it offers a persuasive and powerful tool for understanding man/environment relationships. Is it too fanciful to see the Friends of the Earth as a sect? It is certainly strong group and anti-prescription: its members have tried to avoid any centralized and hierarchical structure, relying rather on strong local groups. And they are certainly suspicious of experts. By contrast, both science and the civil service are caste-like. Science is highly prescribed, with highly institutionalized rules and procedures for making knowledge claims and an elaborate system of rituals for conferring status.[7] Its prevailing dogmas are safeguarded by a high priest-hood, legitimated by the treasury of good words and the lives of the saints whose names are daily reverenced through eponyms (for example, Boyle's law, ohms, farads).

What the theory says is that structure is the clue to cosmology. Those who have been through the long apprenticeship and have passed the initiation ceremonies of science see the world in a particular way. For scientists, nature is law-like. Their job is to discover the rules, to safeguard the doctrines of knowledge and to respect the recognized authorities. Similarly, the civil servants live in a rule-governed world, though their rules are in the files. Perhaps there is a psychological dimension to becoming a member of a caste.[8] It is certainly plausible to argue that those who do not like the restrictions of caste or the insecurities of the market are likely to try to move to a more congenial environment. The important point is that those who live in castes live in different worlds from sectarians and Big Men. The sects have little respect for authority, other than that of the group. The castes by contrast have a high regard for legitimate authority. The castes are risk-avoiders, taking care not to breach the rules and to follow prescribed procedures. The Big Men are pragmatic: they will form alliances with the high priesthood of science and government but only where they think it will pay. It is not reverence for science as such which underlies their provisional support, but rather its promise of powerful magic. If the rule-governed world of science urges caution, the imperatives of the market place push in the opposite direction. And it is no good the Big Men borrowing the authority of science when it suits them to attack the sectarians. For the sects, there is no priesthood. The sectarians can see through the strategies of the market place. They too have little respect for authority, especially when they see it to have been bought.

VALUES, COSMOLOGIES AND CONTEXTS

But in complex industrial societies, individuals operate in a variety of contexts. And they differ too in the importance which they attach to each domain — for some, it is work which is most salient, for others, family life. Moreover, they have some measure of freedom in choosing social contexts. And to make the picture even more complex, if social structures set limits to the range of possible beliefs, it is also true that individuals can and do construct ideal social structures or utopias as reactions against existing social realities. So, on the one hand social contexts set limits to the range of possible beliefs. But as individuals move into different social structures, so cosmologies change. Michael Thompson (1979b), for example, found that the Sherpas joining the Everest expedition became risk-takers. Back in the constraint of their village communities, strong group bonds restrained risk-taking. So the same individuals could be risk-takers or avoiders according to context. And the concept of cosmology does not have quite the same significance as paradigm. Cosmologies change with contexts, whereas we have argued that paradigms are resistant to change.

None of this really tells us much about values and preferences. It is one thing to be constrained to see the world in a particular way; it is quite another to like what you see and experience. We need then to try to push the explanation back a step further, and to return to the evidence of the survey. How do we account for the fact that environmentalists are much more likely to be employed in occupations which place a premium non-material values? Do their values reflect the moral imperatives of their day-to-day lives? Or is it that strongly held values have played a part in pointing them towards careers which emphasize 'post-material' values and which are congruent with their social ideals?

All the evidence points to the second explanation. Inglehart (1977) found that public post-materialists attached more importance to 'working with people you like' and 'a feeling of accomplishment', whereas public materialists tended to choose 'a good salary' and 'a safe job' as things which are most important in a job. Rosenberg (1958) showed that those choosing occupations such as real estate, finance, sales promotion and business, attached a high weight to extrinsic rewards such as status, security and money, and a low weight to self-expresson. By contrast, those preferring careers in architecture, drama, and advertising attached importance to self-expression, and those in social work, teaching and natural science gave a low weight to extrinsic rewards. And those who get to the top in business are more likely to be strongly committed to the goals and values of the market place. A cross-national survey of managers in 15 nations including Britain and the U.S.A. found that those who advanced most rapidly were least willing to spend to eliminate pollution: the only exceptions were Japan, Denmark and Italy (Bass and Eldridge 1973).

A small pilot survey of undergraduates at Bath University confirms the strong association between values, choice of course, and intended career. Undergraduates in social sciences differed markedly from engineers and management students in their support for post-material values and lack of support for economic individualism. The great majority (75%) of social science students were intending careers in the non-market sector, while engineers (81%) and management students (87%) planned to work in the market sector. And there were no significant differences between first and final year students. Such evidence lends very strong support indeed to the view that it is values which underlie choice of different university courses with different career implications (Table 3.1).

Table 3.1. Values, university course and career intentions

	Social scientists (N = 76)	Engineers (N = 62)	Management (N = 64)
Post-material values:	%	%	%
mean scale score	11.6	7.7	7.0
Economic individualism:			
mean scale score	47.4	63.4	63.2
Intended career sector:			
market	13.2	76.7	87.5
non-market	75.0	3.2	0.0

market sector. And there were no significant differences between first and final year students. Such evidence lends very strong support indeed to the view that it is values which underlie choice of different university courses with different career implications (Table 3.1).

So it is this which most probably accounts for the distribution of values between environmentalists and industrialists. It certainly makes sense of the link between the occupations of environmentalists and their values and social ideals. Environmentalists will try to choose occupations congruent with their public post-material values and social ideals. In particular, they tend to choose occupations which do not involve direct commitment to the goals and values of industrialism, and which are congruent with their generally anti-industrial sentiments. This is consistent with Parkin's conclusions from his study of activists in the Campaign for Nuclear Disarmament. 'The occupational location of radicals, results from their desire to avoid direct implication in the capitalist economic system' (Parkin 1968 p.157). And it is further strengthened by follow-up studies of student activists involved in protest demonstrations during the 1960s (Fendrich and Tarleau 1973, Fendrich 1974). The activists were found ten years later to be 'concentrated in the knowledge and human service industries. They had rejected careers in business or the professions that offer the extrinsic rewards of money, status and security and were concentrated in teaching, social services and creative occupations.' But congruence between occupations and values is possible only for those for whom a choice of occupation is a reality. Environmentalists have received an above-average education. And it is this we would argue that enables such a high proportion to choose occupations congruent with their values and ideals. But this is by no means the case for the majority, for whom work is of necessity instrumental as a source of income rather than self-fulfilment. Hence, the absence of any strong connection between occupation and values for the general public.

IDEOLOGIES AND UTOPIAS

But there is a danger that in discussing trends and patterns, we may paint too simple a picture, too black and white when in reality there are shades of grey. The congruence between paradigms and occupations is discernible but not clear cut. Many environmentalists are in occupations which are at odds with their values and beliefs. Yet their costmologies correspond to their ideal world rather than to their actual experience. This point came to us forcefully when pondering over our taped interviews with a number of environmentalists. We were struck by one interview which showed up a marked discrepancy between environment and cosmology.[9] It was a picture of a social world with weak group ties and consultants. Yet the person's world view was one which laid great emphasis on community and group. So cosmologies may be reactions against actual social structures and relate rather to a more desirable social structure — a utopia. But the word utopia is not being used here in the sense of an unattainable dream: rather it is a set of beliefs about how society should really work. It is a view which says the existing map is wrong: it is both a set of beliefs about how the world can really work as well as an evaluation that the alternative social structure is better. So the cosmologies of environmentalists are utopias in the sense that they are beliefs about more desirable social structures. To use Mannheim's distinction, ideologies are beliefs which justify existing social arrangements, while utopias justify change. But even for the industrialists this cosmology does not necessarily correspond precisely with their real world. Their world is not as free from prescriptions as they would like it to be: their map is one which points to more scope for individual initiative, more risk and higher rewards. Yet the link between structure and cosmology remains: beliefs about what the world *ought* to be like set limits to the range of possibilities. Culture is not infinitely variable: if risk and reward is the engine which drives the system, then other possibilities are ruled out.

VALUES, INTEREST AND IDEOLOGIES

The analysis is pushing us further back. However we try to account for different cosmologies and paradigms, we cannot escape from the centrality of values. The paradigms of environmentalists and industrialists are more than sets of beliefs about how the world works: they are also strongly held views that one kind of world not only *works* better but *is* better than another. And we have looked at evidence which points strongly to the conclusion that values influence the search for congenial social environments. So, we still need to explain the differential commitment to material or non-material values, which seems to be central to the acceptance or rejection of the dominant social paradigm. For example, if it is true that differences in values and ideals play a part in influencing choice of occupation, then we have to explain why it is that a possibly increasing proportion of young people are turning away from the dominant social paradigm and embracing post-material values. A favourite explanation is to blame the decline in the spirit of free enterprise on the influence of the universities and other forms of higher education, especially departments of social sciences. But as we have seen in Chapter 2, education is not directly related to values or politics. Our preliminary evidence also suggests that first-year students in the social sciences are already more committed to post-material values. So we need to look to the earlier stages of the socialization process.

Here, Inglehart's (1977) work on value formation and change is important. His original thesis was that there has been a change in the value priorities of politics in Western Europe since 1945, from acquisitive to post-bourgeois values, which he subsequently described as a change from material to post-material values. It is his scales for measuring these changes to which we referred in Chapter 2. His evidence is that there are marked generational differences. Support for post-material values is significantly stronger among those brought up during the period of post-war peace and prosperity. The sources of change he attributes largely to adolescent socialization.

The theory is essentially psychological, and derives from the work of Maslow. Inglehart's explanation of differential support for material values is quite simply that people 'tend to place a higher value on whatever needs are in short supply.' To go beyond such a simple explanatory scheme, he states, 'the work of Abraham Maslow is particularly suggestive' (Inglehart 1977). Briefly, Maslow argues that needs are pursued in a hierarchical order according to their relative urgency for survival. As the basic physiological needs for survival are met, so higher order needs for love, belonging, esteem and self-actualization become increasingly important.[10]

We subjected our data to rigorous analysis to see whether the Maslovian perspective applied. But we found that none of the usual variables (age, income, and education) which explain support for post-material values could account for the large differences *between* our groups (Table 3.2). Though we did not ask the industrial sample to indicate their salary bands, the source of the sample ensured that we tapped only those in relatively senior, and by inference, well-paid posts. Indeed, it is a reasonable assumption that the industrial sample were better off than the environmentalists. And yet they strongly support material values. Our industrial sample were also highly educated. Indeed, rather more held university degrees than environmentalists. There were no differences between graduate and non-graduate environmentalists or industrialists, while marked differences persisted between the groups after controlling for education (Cotgrove and Duff 1981).

What is even more interesting is the pattern of replies from our sample of trade union officials. Support for post-material values was particularly strong, comparable to that of the environmentalists. But they also gave strong support to three of the four material items, similar in this case to the industrialists. Their strong support for post-material values is at first sight problematic. But if we look more closely at the specific items in the post-material list, we see interesting differences between the groups. Trade unionists stand out in the

Table 3.2. Post-materialism scale items (percentage assigning 'high priority')

	Environ-mentalists	Public	Nature conserva-tionists	Indust-rialists	Trade unionists
Material goals					
Maintaining a high rate of economic growth	2	46	38	44	29
Making sure that this country has strong defence forces	12	41	38	18	45
Maintaining a stable economy	50	70	71	70	68
Fighting rising prices	42	78	65	71	68
Post-material goals					
Giving people more say in important government decisions	42	42	13	42	27
Progressing toward a less impersonal, more humane society	71	48	37	65	57
Seeing that people have more say in how things get decided at work	33	31	7	60	18
Progressing toward a society where ideas are more important than money	54	35	15	43	34
n =	(423)	(275)	(218)	(285)	(289)

importance they attach to participation at work. They also share with the public and with environmentalists support for participation in government. By contrast, the industrial sample rejected these items as goals for society. A possible clue is again to be found in important differences in occupational roles. We classified occupations not only according to whether they were located in the market sector, but also according to whether they carried with them the exercise of authority and control over others, subordination, or relative autonomy. The combined picture is given in Table 3.3. Industrialists stand out as being in positions of authority (79%). And environmentalists are also remarkable for the high proportion (46%) in autonomous occupations. Of the trade union officials, 76% were classified as in dominant occupational roles. But previous work experience, political socialization, and the goals of the movement in which they work all emphasize participation as an important value.

Two conclusions emerge. Firstly, Maslow's linear theory that higher-order needs emerge when lower-order needs are satisfied does not fit the data for trade union officials who were remarkable for their strong support for both material and post-material goals. Secondly, their emphasis on participation makes more sense when it is interpreted against the background of the interests generated by their relation to the authority structures of industry. To hark

Table 3.3. Occupational sectors of environmentalists compared with samples of public, industrialists and trade unionists

	En-viron-mental-ists		Public		Indust-rial-ists		Trade union-ists	
Market	%	%	%	%	%	%	%	%
Dominant	11		12		72		67	
Subordinate	10		35		—		15	
Autonomous	13	34	7	54	5	77	1	83
Non-market								
Dominant	6		2		7		9	
Subordinate	26		14		—		5	
Autonomous	33	66	30	46	16	23	3	17
		100		100		100		100
		($n = 350$)		($n = 203$)		($n = 206$)		($n = 260$)

back to our previous discussion of environments and cosmologies, trade unions fit nicely into the category of castes. Their members seek protection from the marketeers by moving towards strong group and strong prescription. It is group solidarity plus protective rules which provide some measure of insulation. Hence, too, their concern with safety and the regulation of risk. They wish to protect themselves from the risky ventures of the marketeers.

THE DECLINE OF THE BUSINESS CULTURE?

Whatever the explanation, there is little doubt about a shift in the ethos of industrial societies; a decline in support for the business culture and protestant work ethic. The evidence of generational differences in support for post-material values is now well established (Dalton 1977). A comparison by Hildebrandt and Dalton (1978) between age cohorts experiencing varying degrees of prosperity confirms that generational changes have persisted into the 1970s. Inglehart reports a comparative study of six nations using the same set of questions in 1970, 1973, and 1976. The year 1973 saw a marked deterioration in confidence in western societies. Yet despite a period from 1971 of exceptional inflation and economic recession unprecedented since the 1930s, support for post-material values showed little change. But this net result conceals changes within age groups. The youngest group, 15–24, declined from 24% post-materialist in 1970 to 20% in 1976. However, this is largely offset by an increase in the 25–34 group from 13 to 16%. Despite this decline, the generational differences remain marked. Moreover, the slight increase in support for post-materialism in the older age cohorts tends to discount the notion that post-materialism is largely a life-cycle phenomenon, and that when the young settle down and acquire responsibilities they will shift to material values (Inglehart 1977). Follow-up studies of student activists have found that they had not 'matured' into taking a more moderate position, nor become disillusioned, but had retained their radical commitment (Fendrich 1974).[11]

How then can we account for what appears to be a major change in world views among some sections of industrial societies? Peace and prosperity provide the conditions which make possible a shift of social ideals (Tallman and Ihinger-Tallman 1979). A certain level of material security may well constitute a threshold beyond which non-material values surface. But this does not explain why some from secure and well-to-do homes shift their priorities to post-material values and goals, while others as affluent and well-educated pursue careers dedicated to material goals. Our data cannot provide the answer. We can only construct a tentative explanation as a basis for further research.

Our first point is to draw attention to the pull of aspirations and ideals as well as to the push of needs. Economic and material values and goals are obviously central in industrial societies. Indeed, what differentiates industrial societies from traditional is the hegemony of economic values and institutions, and the systematic and rational organization of social life in their pursuit. But however much the sub-systems of the family, health, education and welfare function within the context of the overriding economism of industrial capitalism,[12] they remain the carriers[13] of non-economic goals and values. In this sense, the alternative society is with us now, and functions (somewhat uneasily) within the framework of an industrial market society.[14] Those who are most aware of and exposed to the conflicts of values are those who operate outside the market place—especially in the personal service professions and creative arts.[15] It is here that personalist values predominate. And it is in such occupations that those who give priority to non-economic values can find a congenial milieu. It is from this context that those who wish to assert non-economic values can take a stand in defence of an environment which they see to be threatened with destruction precisely by unbridled economism.

The rejection of the primacy of economic and material values is part of a more general world view which is critical of the institutions and practices of industrial capitalism; with its emphasis on economic individualism, and the centrality of market mechanisms. Hence the alignment of post-materialists with the left, not because the left would necessarily share their rejection of economism, but because they have nowhere else to go. Indeed, a significant proportion of environmentalists reject the left/right dimensions in politics entirely as irrelevant to their political objectives precisely because parties of the left are also committed to economic growth and the dominance of material goals (Table 3.4). On the other hand, for those who have a stake in the production of goods and services in the market place, material values serve to legitimate and justify their activities. Support for material values is closely tied to their personal interests. Materialism and post-materialism are tied to interests and ideals and are not simply reducible to psychological needs.

Our data then underline and emphasize the ideological significance of values which relate to political and social goals. Their generation and distribution

Table 3.4. Post-materialism scale scores*

	Environmentalists			Sig-ni-fic-ance	Public			Sig-ni-fic-ance	Industrialists		
	Mean	Standard deviation	N		Mean	Standard deviation	N		Mean	Standard deviation	N
Total sample	59.02	14.54	430	***	44.74	11.07	274	***	38.56	12.23	215
Under 21	64.06	13.25	22	***	47.44	9.72	22	—	—	—	0
21–30	61.05	11.83	121	***	47.34	13.59	54	—	—	—	0
31–40	60.58	14.50	104	***	46.81	10.47	46	N.S.	41.61	16.14	6
Over 40	56.32	15.86	181	***	42.75	10.05	143	***	38.47	12.19	207
Male	N/A			—	44.38	11.15	144	—	N/A		
Female	N/A			—	45.29	11.11	122	—	N/A		
First degree	60.03	12.18	195	***	38.56	17.33	13†	*	39.57	12.88	122
No first degree	60.84	11.36	117	***	46.39	9.53	58†	***	38.14	11.70	39
Up to £2000 pa	61.55	11.77	69	***	47.48	11.61	62	—			
£2001–£4000 pa	61.13	11.84	128	***	42.71	9.02	87	—			
£4001–£6000 pa	59.57	15.73	95	***	45.81	11.33	38	—	N/A		
£6001–£8000 pa	57.21	15.00	62	N.S.	50.57	20.39	11	—			
£8001 +	53.26	14.33	45	—	N<5						
Market	59.97	12.09	125	***	43.80	10.29	116	***	37.13	11.20	160
Non. market	60.69	11.74	230	***	46.68	11.97	97	N.S.	43.81	14.31	48
Dominant	59.47	12.28	63	***	46.98	15.30	31	***	37.67	11.15	165
Subordinate	61.21	12.05	131	***	43.93	9.03	102	—	N<5		
Autonomous	60.07	11.37	162	***	45.58	11.84	75	*	41.74	15.15	42
Market, Dominant	58.05	12.34	40	***	43.75	13.54	24	N.S.	36.95	11.02	149
Subordinate	63.66	12.06	35	***	43.66	9.24	71	—	N<5		
Autonomous	59.04	11.18	47	***	41.52	9.68	14	N.S.	38.44	14.06	10
Non-Market,											
Dominant	61.79	12.31	22	N.S.	60.00	19.69	5	N.S.	44.58	10.73	15
Subordinate	60.67	12.01	92	***	44.98	8.85	28	—	N<5		
Autonomous	60.36	11.43	114	***	46.52	12.16	61	N.S.	42.77	15.54	32
Left	69.94	8.02	63	***	52.68	16.39	14	—	N<5		
Mildly left	62.14	10.04	123	***	51.97	12.08	38	N.S.	53.75	8.37	15
Centre	55.68	10.31	82	***	42.69	9.20	53	*	38.69	11.12	34
Mildly right	50.71	10.01	53	***	42.81	9.62	50	**	37.21	9.98	98
Right	44.79	11.43	15	*	36.98	11.93	24	N.S.	33.21	11.06	43
No position	64.16	11.47	66	***	44.28	8.59	59	*	37.22	15.27	11

*Post-materialism scale score calculated as sum of Likert scores (range 1–5) on eight Inglehart items, converted to a percentage. 'Material' items were recoded so that a high score corresponds to increasing priority for post-material goals.
†Bath only sampled.
N.S. = not significant   * = $p < 0.05$
                           ** = $p < 0.01$
                          *** = $p < 0.001$

cannot be explained simply in terms of need satisfaction or deprivation. Material needs are met within the context of specific social arrangements. The institutions and priorities of industrial society exact a price, in terms of personal relationships, the destruction of primary group loyalties and values, and humanly unsatisfying and alienating work. Entered into by most as an instrumental source of income and security, these institutions are centralized, hierarchically structured, imperatively coordinated, and requiring the application of specialized knowledge beyond the comprehension of the individual. It is the reaction against the costs of materialism which lies at the root of opposition to industrial society. To the environmentalists, commitment to economic growth is seen as the imperative which generates the negative aspects of industrialization. The rejection of the hegemony of economic values and economic individualism has an ideological significance which goes far beyond the satisfaction of material and security needs in an affluent society, and the search for personal fulfilment and self-actualization. It is this political dimension of value change which is important and which cannot be reduced to need satisfaction and deprivation. The commitment of the environmentalists to post-material values is part of a more general ideology which legitimates and justifies a quite different social ideal.

CULTURE AND SOCIETY

Any explanation of changing beliefs and values must then go beyond the view that political socialization can be explained somewhat mechanistically as mainly a response to material conditions. What this cannot account for are the differential responses of different sections of the community enjoying comparable material conditions. Our data reinforce the view that the process of change must be located well back in adolescence. The dramatic difference is between environmentalists and industrialists of all ages. Affluence may well reduce the primacy of economic values. But those who positively embrace post-material values are likely to have been exposed more strongly to such alternative values—with one or both parents working in the non-market sector, or left of centre in politics (Parkin 1968, Braungart 1971). It is in such homes in particular that the young will be exposed to aspirations and ideals for a different kind of society, and in which the institutions and values of industrial capitalism are looked at in a more critical light.[16]

This interpretation is reinforced by researches on the family backgrounds of campus radicals in the late 1960s. Flacks (1971) found a continuity between the basic values and aspirations of new-left activists and their parents. Both were hostile to the competitive status-oriented individualism of bourgeois culture; both sought a way of life which emphasized self-expression, humanism and community; both were substantially disaffected with the political system. Flacks traces the emergence of a new kind of middle class family: less authoritarian and hierarchical; more child-centred and democratic. It is in such families that the new character structures have been moulded, encouraged to pursue individuality and personal autonomy (Flacks 1971 pp.226–230).

Any expansion of employment in the non-market sector could well operate in the same direction. Young people considering such careers, especially those who have the opportunities opened up by higher education, can embrace post-material values as part of the process of anticipatory socialization through identification with their future roles. Those who in recent years have aimed at careers in social work, teaching, or medicine have been able to attach more importance to non-material values including self-actualization, and the enjoyment of a measure of autonomy. By contrast, those aiming at careers in the generally hierarchical structures of industry must expect authority and subordination. And those whose career expectations are confined to the assembly line or routine clerical work can hardly realistically expect self-actualization in their daily lives. But the increase in the numbers of technicians and semi-professionals applying knowledge in work situations requiring an element of autonomous judgement could well challenge the traditional bases of authority based on a hierarchical division of labour (Friedson 1973). And the significance of the growth of higher education may well be that it has increased the possibility of choice.

The general thrust of this discussion indicates that values are formed during adolescence and that any fundamental changes in values must await the slow process of generational change. But this does not rule out the possibility of some measure of subsequent change reflecting adult experience. Rokeach (1974) measured a shift in values between 1968 and 1971 away from material concerns towards increases in the importance of non-material values such as a world of beauty, which he suggests reflects the increasing saliency of ecological issues. Such changes were admittedly mainly confined to white Americans in their twenties. He was also able to achieve changes in values by feeding objective information about inconsistencies in subjects, values and attitudes. This he argues can arouse states of self-dissatisfaction which result in long-term changes in values and behaviour (Rokeach 1974). Such evidence points to the possibility that programmes of information and education can have more immediate, if limited, impact.

All the evidence points to a generational shift in the culture of society. It is possible that the pendulum may swing back, and we could possibly witness a reassertion of material values and the work-ethic. But it is equally possible that despite temporary perturbations, the long-term drift is away from any strong moral commitment to the business culture. And the evidence of substantial levels of unrest among the young in the affluent capitals of Europe supports this view (*The Times* 28/4/81).

NOTES

1. Our use of the term paradigm seeks to maintain a distinction between knowledge and beliefs and their use as ideologies to legitimate and justify actions. But this is not to deny the possibility that paradigms reflect interests and are shaped by social experience. We need to distinguish between the social factors which shape the construction of knowledge and beliefs (and not even science is exempt from such influences) and the use of knowledge and beliefs, including scientific knowledge, to legitimate and justify action.

2. For an example of the use of this approach to explore opposition to science, see S. Cotgrove 1978a.
3. The association could have been stronger had we obtained a purer sample. Twenty-three per cent were employed in non-market sector occupations. This is because our sampling frame included, for example, lecturers in colleges and universities.
4. Marsh argues that dissatisfaction with the material aspects of their job is evidence that post-materialists are also materialists. But this is consistent with Herzberg's two-factor theory of motivation: that pay and security (contextual factors) are sources of dissatisfaction, rather than positive satisfaction, while self-actualization is a source of positive satisfaction. Hence it is quite possible to be concerned about the material aspects of a job in order to remove a source of dissatisfaction. This does not necessarily imply 'materialist' motivation, however (Herzberg 1968).
5. Mary Douglas (1970) labelled these dimensions as 'grid' and 'group'. We have replaced 'grid' by 'prescription' as a more easily understood descriptive concept. We are particularly indebted to Michael Thompson for the development of these perspectives on risk and pollution. I have borrowed the labels 'caste' and 'sect' from him.
6. I am indebted to Michael Thompson for developing this argument.
7. It may be that science holds particular attractions for those who feel the need for a secure and ordered world. Those who embrace the role of scientist tend to be predominantly firstborn or only children, to have experienced isolation in childhood, and to have rejected parental religious beliefs. Science offers an identity in a social system with a highly institutionalized route to membersip of a close-knit community, and with an authoritative cosmology.
See Cotgrove and Box, 1970, Chapter 3.
8. If we ignore the downcastes it is not because we are indifferent to their plight, but simply because this is not the place.
9. This interviewee has since changed his job to one which fits his cosmology.
10. Although Inglehart explains support for post-material values mainly as a function of adolescent socialization, he agrees that some change in basic values may take place during adult life.
11. 'The average age of the Bolshevic leadership in 1917 was 39, but the average age at which these men first . . . defined themselves socially as revolutionaries, was 17' (Abrams 1970). This includes a more extended discussion of generational differences.
12. It can be argued that the overriding commitment to economic and material values and goals of industrial societies (both market and command economies) generates a series of imperatives. Parsons' pattern variables can be seen not so much as the alternatives facing all societies, but as a reflection of the values necessary in industrial societies, and in which hegemonic values reduce problems to technical/instrumental rationality. See Habermas (1971, p.91). The counter-culture's promotion of expressive values is thus a challenge to industrialism in which expressive values must be subordinated to material values.
13. For an exploration of the notion of groups as carriers of world-views see Mannheim (1953) and Cotgrove (1978a).
14. Marxist theorists would argue that such sub-systems are all part of the repressive state apparatus and function to ensure the reproduction of labour. Though there are undoubtedly pressures to ensure that the educational system is harnessed to serving the needs of industry, this is an over-deterministic view, which fails to take account of the operation of educational values in opposition to purely market/economic values.
    The sociology of the professions has grappled with this problem: professional values and codes of conduct can be reinterpreted from this perspective as attempts to protect non-market sub-systems from the intrusion of inappropriate market

values and criteria. The commercialization of medicine would and does raise obvious problems.

15. The emergence of radical movements wihtin the professions are evidence of such conflicts of values and the attempt to assert alternative values. See Halmos (1973).

16. A five-nation comparison between the values of adolescents and their parents found considerable national differences. In Britain, the association was close; in Germany there was marked polarization. But in Germany, the parents were markedly more material and less post-material than the British sample (Jennings *et al.* 1979).

CHAPTER 4

Industrialization and its Discontents

The claimed benefits of industrialization are evident to most and do not need celebrating here. Increases in material well-being, in health and welfare are believed by many to be sufficient justification. And the association between economic advance and democracy is well documented, though controversial (Bowles and Gintis 1978).[1] If this chapter concentrates on the negative aspects of industrialization, it is because this is necessary in order to understand the dissatisfactions and discontents which have surfaced in the environmentalist movement. No attempt will be made to draw up any kind of even-handed balance sheet or to come to any conclusions as to the desirability or otherwise of industrialization. The object is simply to analyse those aspects of industrial society which have become the focus for discontent, and to try to understand the sources of support for changing values and beliefs.

It is not easy to distinguish between what has been described as the 'unacceptable face of capitalism', and those features of modern societies which are the inescapable accompaniments of industrialization, whatever its political complexion — socialist, communist, capitalist, or some mixture of state and private enterprise. Much of the discontent as we have seen is with the institutions of capitalism: with the dominance of the market, and with economic individualism. Capitalism is used here as a purely descriptive term to refer to those societies in which the major part of the means of production is in private hands, and in which the market plays a dominant role in decisions on production and distribution. But state socialist societies share one characteristic with capitalism; they too are cornucopian, dedicated to the creation of wealth. Indeed, they are desperately trying to beat the west at its own game. And in the process, they too have faced major environmental problems (Komarov 1978).

It is rather more difficult to characterize industrialism and industrialization.[2] The application of energy, the use of machines and the large scale organization of production in factories are certainly among its central features (Giddens 1973, p.141). But 'machinofacture', the production of material goods, and the provision of supporting services such as transport, have never accounted for much more than about one-third of the total employment since the nineteenth century (Gershuny 1978). Nevertheless, it is growth in the production and distribution of goods and services which is now the dominant goal of industrial society. What above all distinguishes modern from traditional societies is the overriding importance attached to economic and material goals and values, and the rationalization of all conduct for economic ends (Weber 1930).

THE RISE AND FALL OF ECONOMIC GROWTH[3]

Although economic goals predominate in industrial societies, priorities have periodically changed. Above all, the importance attached to economic growth as the central political objective for economic policy is relatively recent, dating from the late 1950s. In the period following World War II economic policy was dominated by concern for stability and security, with full employment as the prime objective (Arndt 1978). It was during the subsequent decade that emphasis shifted increasingly to growth.

The influences underlying this change in the climate of economic thought were complex, but the cold war threat from the growing economic and military potential of the U.S.S.R. was an important factor, reaching a stage bordering on hysteria when the U.S.S.R. launched its first Sputnik. Gradually, growth came to be seen as the panacea for the major current ailments of western economies—under-employment, inflation, balance of payments difficulties, and the financing of redistribution and welfare. This preoccupation was strengthened by the emerging international rivalry from the rapidly growing economies of Japan and Germany. It was not long before GNP came to be the central indicator of economic health. By 1962, mounting criticisms of constraint on growth for the sake of maintaining the balance of payments finally resulted in Britain following other governments in adopting indicative planning as the central objective.

By the end of the 1960s, doubt and scepticism was growing. The costs and limits of growth were becoming more apparent. Critics questioned too exclusive preoccupation with the rate of growth of GNP, to the neglect of its composition and distribution, and emphasized the economic, social and spiritual cost of economic growth (Arndt 1978 p.84). Galbraith's influential *Affluent Society* (1962) drew attention to the increasing contrast between private affluence and public squalor. Growth had failed to eliminate poverty, while serious inadequacies in public provision for health, education, housing and transport persisted. E. J. Mishan's *The Costs of Economic Growth* (1967) was a powerful tract for the times. He was particularly critical of the negative impact of growth on amenities. He attacked too the erosion of the countryside, the 'uglification' of towns, pollution, and the destruction of our natural heritage. There was a similar disenchantment in the developing countries and for much the same reasons—that mere growth had failed to contribute much to the solution of problems of unemployment, skewed distribution of wealth, health, life expectancy and illiteracy, leading to an emerging distinction between growth and development.

The rejection of growth by environmentalists and by some sections of the radical left must therefore be seen in context. Firstly, it needs to be emphasized that the primacy of growth over other economic objectives such as stability and full employment is a relatively recent and probably transient phenomenon. Secondly, the decline in confidence in growth as the panacea for the ills of industrial society is not confined to environmentalists. Nor is the view that there are physical and environmental limits to growth, though such arguments have provided powerful weapons for them in their critique of industrialization. And it was the growing realization of the inadequacy of GNP which made it possible for the anti-materialist and anti-industrial philosophy of the student revolt and counter-culture movement of the late 1960s to gain such a sympathetic hearing, and to have such an influence on a whole generation of young.

But any decline in the centrality of growth as the overriding political objective would not necessarily weaken the dominant role of economic goals: it could simply herald a shift of emphasis to stability, or full employment. It is economic goals, not growth specifically, which constitute the central and dominant values of industrial societies.

INDUSTRIALIZATION AND ECONOMIC RATIONALITY

What above all characterizes industrial societies is not only their commitment to the creation of wealth, but equally important is the rational and systematic orientation of action to the pursuit and maximizing of economic values, and the use of economic criteria as the bench-mark for evaluating action and policies. Indeed, for Max Weber the value placed on rationality and the rationalization of social life was one of the central features of industrialization, resulting not only in the elimination of all magic and superstition, but in what he described as the 'disenchantment' of social life; the reduction of all action to the impersonal calculus of means and ends (Gerth and Mills 1948, Weber 1968).

The dominance of economic values and institutions was further strengthened in those industrial societies which developed along capitalist lines by the evolution and strengthening of a free competitive market in goods and services. Indeed, despite the fact that the market is a social and political construct, supported by a legislative framework, it has come to be seen as a natural and self-evident fact, having some kind of independent existence outside political and social arrangements (Gellner 1975). The operation of what appear to be impersonal forces is in reality the institutionalization of economic criteria as determinants of choice and decisions, to the exclusion of non-economic criteria. So the environmental impact of a production process, for example, falls outside regulation by market mechanisms.[4]

The need for a mobile labour force plus the enthronement of the economic calculus of the market place meant that labour too became a commodity in the sense that workers were increasingly forced to sell their labour as a condition for survival. A series of essentially political changes ensured this; the enclosure movement in agriculture, changes in the poor law, changes in the common law relations between master and servant, removed traditional and customary protections and increasingly subjected workers to the imperatives of the market place. In practice, this meant the dissolution of the domestic system of production. Textile workers tried to maintain the kinship relationship within which production had functioned under the domestic system, by going as little colonies to colonize the mills. But in vain. Chidlren were sent off to the spinning mills and wives and adolescents to the power-loom sheds (Dickson 1974 p.74).

Under industrial capitalism workers become instruments of production. And the criteria for employment are efficiency and productivity. Tasks are broken down and fragmented in the interests of efficiency, regardless of the effect on the human satisfaction of work. If, on the one hand, workers are engaged as instruments of production, they too come to see work in essentially instrumental terms, as a source of income and security (Goldthorpe 1968). If pride of craftsmanship still persists despite the pressures of the market place, the dominant characteristic of the work force is an instrumental orientation to work. Jobs are chosen by most primarily as a source of income and security; not because they offer the opportunity for satisfying work or the exercise of human skills and abilities. The worker is alienated from control over both his labour and its product.

COMMUNITY AND FRATERNITY

The rational pursuit of economic goals has no place for sentiment. It is the imperatives of the market place which determine where the factories are to be built, and people must follow the work. The notion of some golden pre-industrial age of village communities dancing round the maypole may well be largely myth (George 1953; Laslett 1965). But industrialization wrought profound changes in the structure of social life, replacing personal relationships and status with the impersonal legal relations of contract. Moral relationships and obligations were dissolved and replaced by the cash nexus. And it was these aspects of social transformation which generated such profound anxieties among sociologists such as Tönnies and Durkheim.

Much of the nineteenth century reaction against economic individualism and utilitarian rationalism was essentially conservative — seeking to conserve what were seen to be important values against the socially disruptive effects of unbridled economism and its consequences in the break-up of medieval communal securities rooted in church, family, and guilds (Nisbet 1970). And it was illiberal in the sense that its concern was with the reassertion of traditional forms of order and hierarchy (Dahrendorf 1967). Indeed, far from being descriptive, the conceptualization of community was heavily coloured by such values and ideological preferences. But as we saw in Chapter 1, the environmentalist movement is also heir not only to such notions of traditional community but to another and quite different reaction to industrialization: the anarchist tradition of Kropotkin, Godwin and Thoreau. Kropotkin, for example, sought to bring about a reintegration of social life in which the local community becomes the basis for small-scale decentralized industry, craft and agriculture. Only under such conditions could individuality flourish.

The emergence of a variety of working class institutions was one reaction. The trade unions were more than just an economic defence mechanism. Above all they emphasized fraternity: members were brothers and sisters, and the father of the chapel symbolized the attempt to build loyalties going beyond the limited ties of the market place. Another reaction was the proliferation of communitarian utopias, seeking protection from the march of industrialization within the sheltering confines of self-sufficient and autonomous communities (Armytage 1961, 1968). The thrust of much utopian literature was explicitly in opposition to industrialization and to the dominance of the machine (Sibley 1973). The resurgence of a commune movement in the late 1960s was then nothing new (Rigby 1974).

TECHNOLOGY, HIERARCHY, AND BUREAUCRACY

The mechanization of production went hand in hand with the increasing fragmentation and division of labour. The assembly line epitomizes the highest development of this process. Complex skills are broken down into relatively simple tasks which can be learned quickly and require little skill or knowledge. And the process continues with the replacement of traditional craft skills in the machine shop by numerically controlled lathes. The other side of the process is the need for coordination. And it is this which results in hierarchical structures to organize the many complex functions and to focus them on maximizing the goals of the firm. Hierarchy in turn demands authority and subordination: managers and managed. The march of industrialization then has meant not only the fragmentation of tasks and the destruction of traditional skills and crafts, but also the loss of independence and autonomy, the subordination of a mass labour force to the discipline and authority of the factory, and more recently, the office (Braverman 1974). It was this which was the source of much of the early opposition to the factory system. 'The weavers entered the factories with great reluctance. They resented the discipline that was being forced on them, having been used to organising their own hours of work. They also resented the way that the factory system affected family relationships . . .'. According to a witness to a Government Select Committee in 1874 'all persons working on the power looms are working there by force because they cannot exist in any other way; they are generally people that have been distressed in their families and their affairs broken up . . .' (Dickson 1974, p.74).

It is this facet of industrialization — the dominance and subordination built into its large scale hierarchical imperatively coordinated structures (Dahrendorf 1959), which is at the core of much of the contemporary reaction. The counter-cultural protest of the late 1960s focused on the repressive character of bureaucratic structures in universities as well as industry, commerce, and government. Some carried the search for liberation to extremes, insisting on total spontaneity, and rejecting any kind of structured or planned action.

It is discontents with hierarchical authority structures which surface in a number of ways within the environmentalist movement: the attack on large-scale centralized structures and the celebration of small as beautiful; a preference for decentralized and relatively autonomous units, and a suspicion and distrust of experts. By contrast with industrialists, environmentalists attach high priority to having more say in government decisions and in how things get decided at work. And they want a society in which there is more emphasis on participation in decisions, and in which the influence of experts is reduced.

INDUSTRIALIZATION, CLASS, AND INEQUALITY

Hierarchy within organizations is of course only one facet of the more general inequality of the distribution of power, influence, and rewards in industrial societies. And at the level of society, it is these which underlie class and stratification. Indeed, one influential sociological theory argued that stratification is both necessary and desirable. The distribution of unequal rewards, they argue, performs the primary and necessary function of motivating individuals to fill the various positions required by the division of labour and to carry out the necessary duties. Inequality, it is claimed, is the device 'by which societies ensure that the most important positions are filled by the most qualified persons' (Davis and Moore 1945).[5]

There are serious sociological objections, certainly to the original statement of the functional necessity for stratification, and few sociologists would now accept that it is more than a partial approach to an understanding of inequality. The problems, of course, are as old as society, and not confined to industrialized societies. But they take on a special significance. Whatever the sociological inadequacies of the functionalist theories of stratification, the belief that unequal rewards are necessary to encourage achievement and efficiency can be instantly recognized as widely accepted and indeed constitutes an integral part of the dominant business culture. The important point is that the theory provides a moral justification for inequality.

Once again, then, we uncover an aspect of industrialization which generates different moral responses. The moral justification for rewards and incentives has been further underpinned by the argument that 'wealth creation' provides the resources for welfare, and the abolition of poverty (Bacon and Eltis 1976). Yet the 1960s saw the 'rediscovery of poverty' and the realization that despite a period of unprecedented growth and affluence, poverty remained an intractable problem. Moreover, it became clear that the major source of inequality was still inherited wealth (Westergaard and Resler 1975), which was less easily justified on moral or practical grounds. In short, inequality is not simply a fact of life whether necessary and avoidable or otherwise. It also raises questions of values. What is important in this context is that support for inequality is strong and morally justified by those who are most closely associated with industry and wealth production. It is a central element in the dominant business culture. This is one more facet of industrialization about which environmentalists are less than enthusiastic. They are less convinced of the justification for differentials and inequality, and would prefer a more equal society.

SCIENCE AND ALTERNATIVE STYLES OF THOUGHT

There is a further major dimension of industrialization which is central to any understanding of contemporary discontents. It has to do with the characteristic way in which individuals in industrial societies think about their world, seek to know, understand and control it. And it is science which has exercised a powerful influence on thinking in industrial societies. This dominant style can be decomposed into two main dimensions (Cotgrove 1978b). Science involves an emphasis on the distinction between subjective and objective, between the observer and an external world, between fantasy and reality, and between subjective states of emotion and imagination on the one hand, and a 'reality' which lies outside the observer which can be known only by observation and reason. This is a very different way of knowing and understanding from that which is prevalent in many other societies, including Asian cultures, which see knowledge and wisdom as residing in a state of inner consciousness (Landes 1969, p.25). The clue to discovering the nature of reality for modern science is to penetrate beneath the surface, and to discover the structure and forces underlying appearance. This requires the development of increasingly powerful instruments to observe and measure. Measuring instruments mediate between the observer and natural objects, providing exact dimensions as far as possible free from subjective bias. Such quantifiable data lends itself to mathematical analysis and the formulation of law-like statements of uniformities and regularities (Figure 4.1).

The great attraction and superiority of science is that it has yielded knowledge of pragmatic value, which can be tested by performance. It provides knowledge which when harnessed to another important element in the industrial world view, the sense of dominance over nature, was to transform man's material environment (Leiss 1972). This again is in marked contrast with the orientation to nature which rules in other cultures — a sense of harmony with nature, or even of a fatalistic submission to the dominance of nature (Kluckhon and Strodtbeck, 1961). Some have argued that this sense of human dominance is derived from the Christian tradition which gave man mastery over all the earth, and dissolved any responsibilities to the spirits of field, wood and stream (White 1967; Landes 1969, p.24). But it is science,

	Objective	Subjective
	Reductionist	*Sensate*
Separation	analysis (linear, deductive)	mysticism
	cognition	sensation
	properties of parts explain whole	reality of inner world of mind: consciousness determines existence
	mediation of measuring instruments	opening mind to direct consciousness
	quantitative	
	abstract thought	escape from constraints of external world
	universal laws	
	Holist	*Romantic*
Integration	synthesis (lateral, inductive)	intuition
	cognition	understanding
	whole is greater than sum of parts	integration of thought and feeling, fact and value
	models and analogues	immediate experience
	quantitative	qualitative
	abstract thought	concrete examples
	universal laws	unique instances

Figure 4.1. Styles of thought

harnessed to man's mastery of his environment, which is seen by many environmentalists to be at the root of our present crisis.

Once again, we can point to the late 1960s as a turning point in the triumphant march of science and technology in the esteem of the western world. Of course, there was nothing especially novel or original about the reaction. Elements in the critique echo those of the nineteenth century and earlier (Whitehead 1967). The more extreme reaction involves a total rejection of science, on two main grounds. Firstly, it is seen to be inescapably linked with repression and domination. Positive knowledge allows no escape: it yields inexorable laws and imperatives, with no place for human will or values. Secondly, its epistemology is seen to be flawed and unacceptable. The attack was many-sided (Roszak 1970). From philosophy, and especially the Kantian tradition, there was a growing questioning of the separation of subject and object and of the possibility of objective knowledge. From within science, and without, there was a growing doubt, firstly as to whether the current epistemology was a valid account of the way in which science in fact operates, and an exploration of the subtle interplay between the subjective and objective.[6] Science came to be seen less as simply holding a mirror to nature, and more as an act of intellectual creativity, in which man comes to construct new ways of seeing and interpreting the world (Polanyi 1958; Kuhn 1970; Holton 1974). More specifically, within biology, there was a challenge to the predominant reductionism, which sought to explain complex phenomena in terms of the fundamental building bricks of nature, especially DNA (Koestler 1972). Some sought to explain or explain away all human experiences, including religion and morals, as ultimately to be found within the complex structures of genetic codes (Monod 1971). Its opponents challenged this approach on the grounds that the whole is greater than the sum of its parts and that nature's secrets can only be wrested by adopting a more holistic perspective, by focusing on the properties of systems and by exploring the relations between parts.

Those who were most opposed to science went further than this. They rejected the notion that knowledge, wisdom, and understanding were to be discovered in some external objective reality and emphasized by contrast the centrality of human consciousness. All barriers to direct consciousness in an inner reality must be removed by cultivating the senses. At its most extreme, this was an essentially Dionysian mode which pursues sensation and ecstasy free from the constraints of 'reason' (Holton 1974).

Again, this discussion underlines the fact that the thrust of industrialization involved preferences and choices which excluded alternatives. The dominant positivist style of thought, with its emphasis on the objective and calculable, met the needs of the bourgeoisie, with their commitment to commodity production and their need for calculability and rationality (Mannheim 1953). Some have gone further and argued for the total rejection of the old literary culture. F. Crick, the distinguished biologist, for example, advised university administrators 'to see that their universities became centres for the propagation of a new culture (science) and not merely tombs for propping up an ageing and dying one' (Crick 1966). The critics of such claims to 'epistemological imperialism' drew attention to the price to be paid by a culture dominated entirely by a scientific positivist style of thought. They argued that it neglected, or even rejected, the inner subjective life of experience and sensation, and in this sense diminished humanity. Partisan support and opposition to science is therefore the expression of a value—a preference for one modality over the other. It surfaces whenever there is debate on the relative importance of arts and sciences, useful knowledge, and relevance. And it is useful knowledge, objectivity, calculability—which is most highly valued by the dominant culture of industrialization.

But there were other more immediately practical issues, particularly relevant to the environment. The nuclear power controversy provides a good example. From the late 1960s there was growing concern around many of the technical aspects of nuclear power—radiation hazards, waste disposal, fast breeder reactors, and the emergency core-cooling systems designed to prevent meltdown in the pressurized-water reactors. In the earlier stages of the programme, there had been little debate on such issues. Indeed, atomic energy authorities had sheltered behind the complexity of the process in maintaining that such issues were highly technical and beyond the competence of public debate.

In this as in other environmental controversies on technical issues, science had been harnessed to support authority and to protect decisions from questioning (Nelkin 1975). Environmentalists and other protesters seeking to extend control over the impact of technology found themselves not only up against what they saw to be impervious bureaucracies, but also denied access to data and information as too technical. And in this scientists were often cast in the role of supporting authority and impervious to questioning. The last decade has provided environmentalists with solid grounds for challenging any uncritical acceptance of scientific expertise. Scientists have been ranged on both sides of debates which are crucial to judgements on risk and safety. Environmentalists have been able to muster expert opinion to challenge industry and government. The controversy over safe radiation, for example served to bring to public notice the fact that on this and other crucial issues, competent and respected scientists disagreed. The outcome of this controversy was that 'safety' levels for radiation were drastically reduced: '. . . the work of two of the AEC's own highly respected radiation experts now supported claims which only a few years before had been considered the work of cranks and charlatans' (Del Sesto 1980 p.152). Scientists are now less likely to be placed on a pedestal of infallibility (Nelkin 1975).

There has then been a growing questioning of the 'objectivity' of science and the disinterestedness of scientists. Whenever knowledge and beliefs are used to justify and legitimize policies and courses of action, science is being put to ideological uses to support particular interests. When scientists give evidence at public inquiries, they are caught up in political debate. Moreover, it can be shown that a substantial proportion of the total scientific effort is related to production and defence, to the relative neglect of research on environmental impacts. Consequently, it is argued, society lacks the necessary scientific intelligence for realistic environmental policies (Schnaiberg 1980).

There is one last aspect of attitudes to science and technology which can be summed up as the 'uses and abuses' debate. This is not concerned with any questioning of the value of science, but rather with the uses to which science is put, and with the social responsibility of scientists for the ethical applications of science. This approach is generally rooted in a critique of capitalism, rather than of industrialization as such. Its more radical supporters argue for a change in the social structures and institutions in a direction which will ensure that science and technology are harnessed to socially useful purposes, and to regulate the more harmful effects of pollution, or the uses of science for inhuman military ends.

In their attitudes to science and technology, the environmentalist movement again exemplifies discontent with a central feature of industrial society. They are less confident in the ability of science and technology to solve our problems, and in the beneficial effects of technology. But more fundamentally, some attach less importance to reason and science and more to subjective experiences.

SYMBOLS AND LEGITIMATIONS

It is in this context then that we can understand the ambivalent and even hostile attitudes of environmentalists towards science and technology. Modern science is inextricably integrated into the structure of industrial society and has flourished because of its contribution to industrialization. Indeed, it has in many respects displaced religion as a source of justification and meaning. The authority of science underpins practices and justifies policies. It is in this sense that science constitutes a major element in the ideology of industrial capitalism (Habermas 1971).

The search for some alternative authoritative basis for environmental values and beliefs explains the widespread appeals to natural symbols in environmentalist literature and debate. In its early stages, and especially in the U.S.A., it was referred to as the 'ecology' movement. Indeed, one of the main journals for the new environmentalism in Britain is still called *The Ecologist*. This particular branch of biology emphasizes the relations between the members of natural communities and the interdependence of species within a habitat. It draws particular attention to ways in which the balance of nature can be upset by human intervention, and hence can provide authoritative backing for environmentalist policies (Catton 1980; Lowe and Worboys 1980). And because it adopts a *holistic* approach, and stresses the systemic properties of natural systems, it has a particular attraction for environmentalists who are critical of what they see as the inadequate reductionist and atomistic approach to the understanding of nature which dominates in the natural sciences, and which has been the basis of what they see as destructive behaviour towards the environment.

Hence, too, the substantial literature which seeks to derive an ethic from nature. Such attempts, of course have a long history. The medieval doctrine of natural law provides an influential example.[7] Recently, the American philosopher Henri Skolimowski (1978) has published a series of papers which seek to derive moral imperatives from the study of natural systems.

Nature is also evaluated differently by many environmentalists. What is natural is seen to be intrinsically good, and preferable to the non-natural, mechanical and artifical. It follows that a purely instrumental attitude to nature which makes natural systems available for human ends is unacceptable. Indeed, some would argue that animals too have rights — not merely to life but also to an adequate quality of life.

THE TECHNOLOGICAL SOCIETY

So powerful is the impact of industrialization on society that it has nourished a widely accepted determinist view: the belief that the inexorable logic of industrialization generates a series of imperatives which leads all industrial societies, whatever their political persuasion, to adopt similar social institutions and practices. This is the view that all industrial societies are converging, and that differences between capitalism and socialism will largely disappear. What is important about this theory is that it locates the forces shaping society in the industrialization process as such, rather than in any specifically capitalist mode of production. And it is technology which is identified as the engine which drives the system. Indeed it is part of the conventional wisdom that the transformation of society which has come to be known as the industrial revolution was the result of a series of inventions: new machines, materials, and sources of energy, which were harnessed by the early entrepreneurs with dramatic results. It is the new technology, it is argued, which leads to the concentration of production in factories so that the machines could be driven first by water and then by steam power. Whatever the variations and elaborations of this account, it is essentially a technological determinist view: that technology generates a series of imperatives, to which society responds. The view is persuasive. There is a remarkable similarity about assembly lines, textile mills, airports, and electrical generating stations throughout the industrial world, regardless of the political context in which they operate.[8]

The most extreme version of this perspective is deeply pessimistic. Ellul (1965) believes society to be in the grip of forces from which it cannot escape. It is a society dominated by technique. Like Weber, Ellul sees the march of technique as inexorable:

'If a desired result is stipulated, there is no choice possible between technical means and non-technical means based on imagination, individual qualities or tradition. Nothing can compete with technical means . . .' (Ellul 1965, p.84).

Now what is important about this perspective is that it talks about technology as though it were an independent force, operating outside the wills and intentions of persons. In recent years, this idea that technology is some kind of neutral force in society has come under increasing attack. It is now argued that technology can only be understood within the context of the relations of production. Machines are invented and developed to meet human purposes and intentions. And these included problems of controlling and organizing a labour force:

'. . . technological innovation was determined, not only by concern for the efficiency of production technology but also by the requirements of a technology that maintained authoritarian forms of discipline, hierarchical regimentation and fragmentation of the labour force' (Dickson 1974, p.64).

So, it is argued, machines were introduced to help create a framework within which discipline could be imposed, and 'as a conscious move on the part of employers to counter strikes and other forms of industrial militancy' (*ibid.*, p.79). For example, increasing the length of spinning mules displaced adult spinners, thereby weakening the factory apprentice system and reducing the spinners' authority. Andrew Ure, writing in 1835, commented on the self-acting mule:

'This invention confirms the great doctrine already propounded, that when capital enlists science in her service, the refractory hand of labour will always be taught docility' (Dickson 1974 p.80).

Such historical examples could be matched by more recent cases. The introduction of numerically controlled machine tools, for example, was in part aimed to increase managerial control (Noble 1978).

The conviction that technology is a neutral and objective force springs from the fact that the values which are incorporated in technological products and which guide and inform the actions of technologists and those who direct their work, are either unrecognized, or simply taken for granted. In the practice of engineering, it is constantly stressed that engineering solutions must be cost-effective and efficient, and that products must be marketable. Given certain assumptions as to values, then such statements are simply reflecting the reality of the context in which engineering is practised. Indeed, the engineers in our sample differed little from senior businessmen in their strong support for material values, and equally important, their low priority for non-material values. It is the unquestioning acceptance of economic values which makes it look as though the march of technology is inexorable. Given a market economy, and given the fact that developments in micro-electronics are likely to be very cost-effective, then such developments may well appear irresistible — regardless of the social cost in terms of unemployment. But switch to a different calculus using different criteria, such as satisfying work, or full employment, then the parameters which guide the engineer, and the resulting technologies could well look different. And it is such values — satisfying, non-alienating work — which environmentalists prefer. Far from being value free, technology is up to its eyes in values.

INDUSTRIALIZATION, TECHNOLOGY, AND VALUES

This brief discussion makes no claim to be a complete analysis of the nature of industrial society. The crux of the argument is that industrialization faces society with choosing some options in preference to others. And choice implies criteria — values. Industrialization then maximizes some values, but at the expense of others. It has been conspicuously successful in 'wealth creation', and has made possible the provision of a level of material and non-material well-being never before known. But in doing so, it has brought about profound transformations in the nature of society. In place of the traditional respect for status and position, modern societies replace contract and achievement. Individuals are valued not for the kinds of people they are, but by what they have achieved. In place of the personal bonds of kinship and community, modern societies substitute impersonal bureaucratic relations, and the cash nexus of the market place. The pursuit of economic goals and efficiency lends moral justification to hierarchy and inequality. And individuals become instruments of production in work which maximizes output at the expense of human satisfaction. In place of the traditional knowledge acquired through experience and practice, modern societies institutionalize the pursuit of knowledge in universities and research institutes. A body of 'objective' knowledge is generated which the ordinary individual finds difficult to understand and from which he feels alienated. More and more issues are decided by experts.

The increasing impact of technology serves to heighten such value dilemmas, and the speed of technological change leaves little time for reflection and absorption. In short, things are far from well with industrial societies. Many feel that we have paid a high price for material well-being. Not all share the view that industrial society is the good society. Nor are they confident that it can solve its problems. Environmentalists in particular are pessimistic about the future of a society which they believe to have squandered its birthright, polluted its environment, and sacrificed human values for the pursuit of material gains.

SOCIAL INTEGRATION AND CONFLICT[9]

What then holds industrial society together? What social forces and mechanisms ensure its continued integration and cohesion? The liberal analysis argues that the individual pursuit of self-interest in a free market will maximize the good of all. Moreover, the impersonal competitive market imposes a system of disciplines and constraints. The cash nexus structures and enforces a system of social relations which ensure the integration and cohesion of society. Individuals are motivated by self-interest and kept in place by the laws of the market. But it is also a moral justification. Inequalities arise not from any injustice in the system but out of natural differences and abilities. Classical liberalism was, and is, both a theory of society and an ideological justification for particular institutional arrangements, rooted in a specific view of human nature. Market capitalism was and is seen as both natural and rational.

The Marxist critique rejected the justice of a system in which the private ownership of the means of production generated inequalities arising out of the unequal bargaining power of labour in the market place. As a consequence, the worker receives only a fraction of the surplus value which he creates: the balance being creamed off to further the process of capital accumulation. The system, therefore, is seen as neither just nor stable. Its maintenance rests on coercive measures. Wage labour is forced labour, and the worker is alienated from both the processes and the product of his efforts.

The rise of social democracy[10] as a political movement and of academic sociology in the latter part of the nineteenth century were each in part a response to dissatisfaction with classical liberalism and Marxism as tools of social analysis and as guides to policy (Room 1979, p.34). Durkheim, Weber and Tönnies were all concerned as the disruptive impact of market capitalism on the traditional social order. For Durkheim, the division of labour threatened old allegiances and the pursuit of self-interest corroded all stable social groupings. Durkheim saw society as essentially a moral entity rooted in moral obligations and allegiances. He was sympathetic therefore to social democratic policies of intervention for the promotion of social justice, because only a just social order would ensure the moral commitment of its members. The task for the state then was nothing less than to promote the moral reconstitution of society.

Weber too challenged the view that the virtues of either the liberal or Marxist versions of a rationally organized society would be sufficiently evident to evoke the freely willed acquiescence of its members (Room 1979, p.36). Such acquiescence, he argued, could not be purely self-interested, but must be rooted in the acceptance of social duties as morally binding. The central task of political leadership is to secure the moral basis of allegiance and, hence, the legitimacy of the system. The dangers of state intervention are the increasing powers of bureaucratic administration. What particularly concerned Weber was the tendency for bureaucracies to rely on the formal rationality of procedural correctness to engender a sense of civic obligation to the neglect of the more fundamental need to win support for the substantive rationality of policies.

A CRISIS OF LEGITIMACY?

The problem is to win the hearts and allegiances of citizens: that is, it is essentially the problem of legitimacy. The reaction against classical liberalism is the search for ways to assert the public good. Various forms of state intervention are seen as necessary to promote a principled moral order, to restore a sense of community and fraternity, in which social cohesion is rooted in a sense of justice. The question that is now being raised is whether social democracy is itself facing a crisis of confidence which amounts to a threat to the legitimacy of politics.

To simplify the argument we can conceive of three main bases for political compliance (Table 4.1). Firstly, and obviously, coercion: the threat of sanctions. Secondly, there is calculative or utilitarian compliance. This rests on the belief that it is in the broad interests of the individual to support the system. Thirdly, there is normative compliance which rests on a belief that the government has a moral right to govern and ought to be obeyed (Etzioni 1961).

It is the second and third of these modes of compliance which are clearly of most importance in democratic societies. It is when the basis of willing compliance weakens that there is increasing need to have recourse to coercive

Table 4.1. Modes of political compliance

Coercive	Compliance forced by threat and use of sanctions: physical punishment, material deprivation, etc.	Power
Calculative/ utilitarian	Compliance voluntary: based on belief that government meets interests and needs (efficacy).	↕
Normative	Compliance rests on belief that government has moral right and ought to be obeyed (legitimacy).	Authority

measures. Indeed, the further governments can move towards the third basis for compliance the better. Calculated self-interest provides only a tenuous basis. Governments need to win mass loyalty and respect for the political system. It is this which ensures the shift from power to authority, that is to *legitimate* power.

This concept of legitimacy is not an easy one to grasp. It is clearly not the same thing as legality. It is after all governments (including the judiciary of course) who in the last analysis determine what is legal. But they cannot guarantee respect for the law or for legal processes. The history of prohibitionist legislation on drink is evidence enough of that. The notion of legitimacy implies a moral judgement — that the action can be justified by appeals to some criteria higher than legality. And this in turn depends on the acceptance of some core of common values (Lipset 1963). The problem of legitimacy is one that faces all governments. The medieval solution was to invoke the doctrine of divine right as the source of authority. Modern governments depend on an extremely complex set of doctrines which include claims to be democratic, to rise above sectional interests in the service of the national interest, as well as to behave constitutionally, according to an accepted set of conventions, plus responsiveness to demands, and efficacy in meeting them. But this rather formal legal/rational basis for legitimacy provides only a relatively weak power to win moral compliance. It lacks the appeal of substantive ideals (Poggi 1978).

As we have seen, since the 1950s governments have increasingly turned to economic growth as a justification for state intervention. But there are signs that the crisis of confidence in social democracy is both deep-seated and widespread. The intervention of the state to both moderate market mechanisms and sustain the economic and social order has spawned a large impersonal and expensive bureaucratic administrative apparatus. This has tended to shunt parliament away from the centre of political life. The executive apparatus functions increasingly without adequate political control, leading to a sense of political impotence (Poggi 1978). Moreover, the rising costs of public sector expenditure have generated a widespread taxpayers' revolt. This is not mainly against welfare as such, but against the wastes, inefficiencies and abuses of what some have described as the 'pocket money society'. Moreover, the massive welfare state apparatus has failed to tackle deep-seated inequalities (Lipset 1980). In short, there are signs of increasing disenchantment with what are seen to be the failures of social democratic policies to generate effective state intervention to achieve prosperity and social justice (Dahrendorf 1980).

What is remarkable about these examples of the main currents of social and political analysis is the way in which their diagnosis of the fundamental problems facing market civilizations resonate with the rhetoric of contemporary environmentalism. Such an analysis underlines the central argument of this study that the new environmentalist movement has provided a focus for crystallizing and expressing anxieties which are endemic to industrial capitalism and are essentially concerned with the moral basis and cohesion of society. The predominantly 'middle class' supporters of the new environmentalism are especially vulnerable and exposed to the stress points in market civilizations. Their occupational roles locate them outside the market place. As teachers, social workers, doctors, research scientists and academics, their roles sensitize them to the limits of economic self-interest, and indeed, to the needs of the casualties of the market place. Hence the hope expressed by many that the professionalization of occupations might provide a means for the humanization of industrial society through the introduction of ethical considerations (Carr-Saunders and Wilson 1933, Halmos 1973). Environmentalists are concerned with moralizing the social order rather than with its revolutionary overthrow. They are symptomatic of a wider failure of market civilizations to win the moral support and allegiance of those who are not its prime beneficiaries.

The rise of 'green' political groups needs to be seen then as part of a more widespread disenchantment with social democracy (Dahrendorf 1980). But the dissent spans the political spectrum. On the right, the taxpayers' revolt is 'probably the revolt of the individual against the iron cage of bondage of the welfare state and the big battalions of business and the unions' (Dahrendorf 1980 p.10). There is a demand for less government, a strengthening of law and order, and resistance to liberalization in education and the media. There are signs too that in some of its manifestations the new right is 'anti-rational' and shares with the counter culture a celebration of emotion (Cotgrove 1978a). The new left wants 'real' equality—that is, equality of results. It wants 'real' participation, involving people fully in the government of their own affairs and favouring mandated or delegate government in preference to representative democracy. What these all share is a loss of confidence in benevolent government which is the central assumption of social democracy (Dahrendorf 1980).

The political manifestations of environmental protest can be seen as expressions of such more fundamental social trends. We turn in the final two chapters to an exploration of the implications of environmental issues for political structures and processes.

NOTES

1. It has been argued, for example, that liberal democracies and free markets have been less successful in achieving economic growth than more dirigiste states (Arndt 1978).
2. It is not the purpose of this discussion to attempt any systematic analysis of competing theories of industrialization, but rather to use them to identify the more fundamental social processes which are at the roots of discontents with industrial societies. Only on this basis can we discuss alternative futures.
3. The analysis which follows draws heavily on Arndt (1978).
4. Hence the need to devise economic strategies to take account of so-called 'externalities' such as pollution. Such social costs are external to the market.
5. For a more detailed exploration of this controversy and a survey of data and theories of stratification, see Cotgrove 1978a Chapter 7.
6. For an example of recent research substantiating the view that scientific knowledge too is socially constructed, see Collins 1979.
7. There are incidentally philosophical objections to any attempt to derive 'ought' propositions from statements of fact—the so-called naturalistic fallacy. See Nowell-Smith 1954, pp.32–34, 180–2, for a discussion of the 'naturalistic fallacy'.
8. A popular and influential version of this perspective is to be found in Kerr *et al.* 1960. For a discussion of the ideological significance of the logic of industrialism, see Plant 1979, pp.165–71.
9. This section draws heavily on Room (1979), Chapter 2, 'The Capitalist Market Society'.
10. Social Democracy refers to a broad political philosophy distinct from Marxism which seeks to moralize rather than displace the market and overthrow capitalism.

CHAPTER 5

Politics and the Environment

In the last decade the awareness of environmental problems has not only increased dramatically, but has taken on a new political significance. Environmentalist groups have been at the centre of protest, locally and nationally, against motorways, airports, and dams, and have vigorously opposed the nuclear power programme in a number of countries. And in the last few years, newly formed 'ecology parties' have captured a sizeable proportion of the votes at elections. The significance of the environment has shifted from a preoccupation with the preservation of the countryside, historic buildings, and local amenities, to become the focus for radical protest.

PARTICIPATION AND PROTEST

But it would be a mistake to see such an increase in protest and direct action as particularly characteristic of environmental issues. On the contrary, the last two decades have witnessed a marked increased in the level of political protest, conflict, and violence (Marsh 1977). And this has been true of all advanced industrial societies. Indeed, it is argued that such phenomena are rooted in much more fundamental transformations whose sources are to be found within the industrialization process itself. The conflict has been between races, over questions of community power, and within industry. The CND movement, Suez, rent strikes, the Welsh nationalist movement, opposition to the South African tour — all are examples of political protests which crossed the boundaries of legality (Benwick and Smith 1972; Carter 1973; Crouch 1977). In short, we can identify a spectrum of political change from a demand for a substantial increase in the level of participation and involvement in decision-making, through an increase in illegal but non-violent direct action, to extreme expressions of violence in pursuit of political aims.[1] Of course, some element of protest, direct action and even violence is endemic even in democratic political systems. The suffragette movement is only one of many examples. What is perhaps surprising is that Britain has occupied such a high place in the league table of protest in recent years, ranking tenth out of 136 countries for the post-war period (Marsh 1977).

If, then, we are to understand the implications of the environmentalist movement for politics, we need to see this against the background of the broader political changes of recent decades, and rooted in more deep-seated social changes. The demand for increasing participation and involvement in decision making is present in all the advanced industrial societies, though its manifestations reflect the different political cultures and institutions within western democracies.[2] It is easy to understand how the environment has come to provide a particular focus for such demands. the impact of technology had generated a growing number of issues—aircraft noise, the need for new reservoirs, new and powerful insecticides and herbicides, motorway development and urban reconstruction, and most recently, the siting of nuclear power stations—all provided issues on which demands for participation have been focused. In short, the increasing and sometimes dramatic impact of technology on the enviroment and the daily lives of citizens has contributed to a growing questioning of the processes by which such decisions are arrived at. But this is not all. The general trend in industrial societies is towards a growth in the scale of organization, and the increasing centralization of decision making. An emerging exasperation with inaccessible bureaucracies has been exacerbated in some countries (e.g. Sweden and later Britain) by organizational changes which have resulted in even greater concentration and the removal of most decisions from the local level to area and regional structures (Nelkin 1977). At the same time, the growing impact and complexity of technology reinforced the inaccessibility of decisions and encouraged an increasing reliance on expert opinion. That is to say, there has been a shift in political decision making to administration and bureaucracy. It is this which has contributed towards the depoliticization of issues such as nuclear power (Nelkin and Pollak 1980b). And finally, the increased involvement by governments in the economy and its supporting infrastructures has encouraged alliances with labour and capital, a trend towards corporatism, and a growing awareness of an increase in state power.

REDISCOVERY OF POLITICS

The prevailing political orthodoxy in the 1950s and 1960s was crystallized in a series of influential and predominantly American studies which presented a model of the political system in which conflict was contained under the umbrella of an overriding consensus.[3] A set of highly institutionalized political structures (parties, pressure groups) and processes (the articulation and aggregation of interests) ensured a high level of political stability, grounded in consensus and legitimacy rather than coercion (Dahrendorf 1959; Dahl 1961; Almond and Verba 1963). This prevailing view was reflected too in the influential writings of Daniel Bell (1962),[4] who drew attention to the exhaustion of the old ideologies. Many went further and argued that the great ideological conflicts of the past were over. The overriding political goal emerged as the pursuit of growth, efficiency and modernization. It was confidently believed that industrial society had within its grasp the good life, and the solution to the personal problems of want, ignorance and disease. Politics was thus reduced to a debate about means rather than ends. The task of politics was increasingly seen to be to harness the expertise of scientists, technologists, economists, and systems analysts to the consensual goal of a cornucopian utopia. This was the politics of technocratic consensus in which politics as the allocation of values becomes replaced by administration as the application of means (Benewick and Smith 1972).

The rumblings of rebellion were apparent in the late 1950s, especially among the young. The Suez invasion generated the first signs of massive political dissent. A few years later, the 'bomb' was the catalyst for the expression of a more generalized sense of political alienation, frustration and cynicism. Faced with what was seen to be a political system deaf to issues outside the defined consensus, direct action was increasingly believed to be the only way of ensuring that the issue would be taken up (Cadogan in Benewick and Smith 1972). The environmentalist movement is heir to the same concerns[5] and shares the same constituency (Taylor and Pritchard 1980).

But the major challenge to the dominant political culture came in the middle and late 1960s, exemplified especially by the student unrest, and the rise of the so-called counter culture. This offered a powerful critique of the hegemonic material values of industrial capitalism, and an attack on its impersonal centralized bureaucratic structures. In place of the protestant work ethic it substituted the ethic of self-realization. The vigour, and in some countries, the ferocity of the movement constituted a fatal rupture to any notion of a consensual civic culture.

The political response was at least a partial recognition of the need for an extension of participation, both in industry and central and local government. Civic and amenity societies, and a variety of special interest groups pressed for and got enquiries and tribunals. Yet such measures failed to satisfy. Inquiries into the routeing of motorways were disrupted on the grounds that the terms of reference were too restricted: that a questioning of the basic political values —of the need for motorways, or increases in energy supply in the pursuit of economic growth—were excluded. Protest, direct action, and in some cases violence has persisted.

LEGITIMACY AND PROTEST

So, how can we explain the increase in political protest and direct action? It is certainly inconsistent with the conventional political widsdom. The dominant view of democracy in Britain attributes its stability to the high level of support for its political institutions, a respect for law and order. That is to say, the system is believed to enjoy a high level of legitimacy. Considerable emphasis is placed on the part played by the electorate as the ultimate sovereign which determines government action and the belief that at elections people are offered a meaningful choice between competing programmes. A corollary is that is is wrong to take part in direct action outside the 'normal' political channels and that those who do are agitators, extremists and trouble-makers. At the same time, it is acknowledged that citizens have a right to demonstrate and engage in collective political protest, though it is unnecessary to assert this right because constitutional channels are fair and effective (Chamberlain 1977).

What then has changed? The researches of Almond and Verba were based on field work in the late 1950s. Although the questions asked differ from those of recent studies, some comparisons can be made. What does emerge is evidence of a very significant decline in what they describe as a sense of civic competence. This is composed of two elements. Firstly, subjective competence is measured by the belief that citizens can actually influence government outcomes, for example, by doing something about unjust regulations. In the Almond and Verba studies, 78% in Britain and 77% in the U.S.A. believed that they could influence local government. Corresponding figures for central government were 62% and 75% (Almond and Verba 1963 p.185). The second component is the sense of administrative competence; that the administration is responsive and will listen to demands. In the U.K., 53% thought that government officials would give serious consideration to their point of view, while 74% gave this answer about the police.

The contrast with the findings of recent researches is marked. Marsh (1977) developed comparable measures. A series of questions were devised to test how far individuals felt able to influence the government and politicians, that is, a sense of personal efficacy. For example, 'Parties are only interested in people's votes, not their opinions'; 67% agreed. He concluded 'Each question attracts a majority view that politics is remote and an unresponsive system run by cynical and aloof politicians' (Marsh 1977 p.115). A second measure aimed to probe what Marsh calls political trust. He concludes 'Political trust is at a low ebb. A clear majority of those responding expressed their belief that Britain is governed and administered by self-interested men (of *both* parties) acting on behalf of a "few big interests", and who cannot be relied upon to do the right thing . . . . Furthermore, fully 70 per cent of the total sample thought "people in politics" were habitual liars.' (Marsh 1977 p.119).[6]

Nor can it be argued that disaffection with the political system is confined to a section of the middle class. CND marchers were predominantly young and well-educated (Parkin 1968). Student activists tended to come from well-to-do homes. And much of the liberatory thrust of the 1960s came from intellectuals, writers and artists. Perhaps such protests are little more than a heady froth, which leaves the solid core of the electorate firm in their deference towards authority? The evidence however is otherwise. A study of predominantly working class rent strikers in the London borough of Barking found that those who paid the rent increases did so not because of any respect for the law, but because they saw no alternative and feared the consequences. Moreover, only a minority of all the population sampled thought that the most effective way to influence the government was through normal political channels (Chamberlain 1977).[7] Not surprisingly, there is evidence of a steady decline of partisan support for the major political parties (Crewe *et al.* 1977).

The reaction to the loss of efficacy of normal channels is also not surprising. The great majority (73%) thought that either there was no effective way (34%) or that collective action, strikes, demonstrations were the only way (37%). Only 2% disapproved of political strikes in opposition to the elected government (Chamberlain 1977). Such evidence is supported by wider studies. Marsh (1977) found substantial support for crossing the threshold from legal to unorthodox forms of political behaviour: 27% would be prepared to go beyond petitions, lawful demonstrations and boycotts to rent strikes, unofficial acts, occupations, and blocking traffic. He concludes 'protest behaviour, far from being the occasional out-bursts of a hopelessly alienated minority (the "rent-a-crowd" theory), is an integral part of British political consciousness and is viewed . . . as a legitimate pathway of political redress by widely differing sections of the community' (Marsh 1977 p.39). Such evidence underlines the conclusion that the last two decades have seen a dramatic decline in political legitimacy. The problem is to account for it.

Such evidence of a general loss of trust and confidence in political processes is reinforced by the results of the international survey. We asked 'How much would you trust the following groups to solve environmental problems?' Out of a list which included industry and trade unions, no great confidence was

Table 5.1. Trust in groups to solve environmental problems

	Little (1-3) %	Great (5-7) %	N
TURST IN GOVERNMENT: ENGLAND			
New Environmentalists	62	14	171
Conservationists	35	31	198
Industrialists	30	34	259
Public	42	27	710
TRUST IN GOVERNMENT: U.S.A.			
Environmentalists	39	18	206
Industrialists	49	17	204
Public	36	24	142
TRUST IN POLITICAL PARTIES: ENGLAND			
New Environmentalists	74	9	171
Conservationists	62	11	200
Industrialists	68	11	260
Public	61	14	710
TRUST IN POLITICAL PARTIES: U.S.A.			
Environmentalists	75	3	207
Industrialists	80	3	203
Public	75	5	141

shown in either governments or political parties (Table 5.1). But industrialists, who give least support to direct action, had marginally more confidence. Confidence is particularly low among the new environmentalists in England, and among all publics sampled in the U.S.A.

Table 5.2. Opportunity to influence environmental policy

	Little (1-3) %	Much (5-7) %	N
ENGLAND			
New environmentalists	52	28	173
Conservationists	59	21	199
Industrialists	55	21	260
Public	74	10	710
U.S.A.			
Environmentalists	33	39	208
Industrialists	43	33	206
Public	62	16	143

Table 5.3. Effectiveness of government action re environment

	Inadequate (1-3) %	Adequate (5-7) %	N
ENGLAND			
New environmentalists	92	2	173
Conservationists	76	11	196
Industrialists	57	22	256
Public	71	8	700
U.S.A.			
Environmentalists	77	8	219
Industrialists	40	35	220
Public	51	14	149

A further question asked 'How much opportunity do you feel you have to influence environmental policy in your community?'. The general picture is similar. No group in the U.K. and U.S.A. felt they had much influence. Here, interestingly, environmentalists felt they had marginally greater influence, reflecting perhaps their experience of some success through pressure group tactics (Table 5.2). Finally, the effectiveness of government action on environmental questions is generally judged to be inadequate, especially by environmentalists (Table 5.3).

PARADIGMS, COMMUNICATION, AND RATIONALITY

Almond and Verba's analysis argues that the high level of confidence in political institutions is rooted in the effectiveness of participation; a belief in high levels of civic competence in the sense that citizens felt that the political system is both accessible and responsive. Two decades later, the evidence points overwhelmingly to a totally different picture. Profound dissatisfaction with access to and influence over decision makers has resulted in demands for meaningful participation and angry frustration at what is often seen to be empty participation which is restricted to administrative details and preempts debate about the fundamental political issues of competing values. Such evidence suggests that the process of political communication is crucial in maintaining confidence in the system. Indeed, one of the outcomes of the recent Windscale Inquiry on reprocessing nuclear waste has been to identify ways in which the presentation of alternative viewpoints was hindered and to suggest ways for improving the structures for participation and communication.

There would seem to be room for substantial improvement in the existing channels, including a questioning of the conventional wisdom. Politicians will argue that it is part of their skill to keep their finger on the pulse of opinion in their constituences. But the processes of perception and interpretation are complex and could well result in distortion. An extensive survey of environmental attitudes and beliefs in the U.S.A., for example, found that there was a discrepancy between what the political leaders believed was the public's rating of the seriousness of the environmental problem and actual public opinion: the public viewing the issues as more serious than the politicians believed was the case (Milbrath 1975, p.41).[7]

But the problem would appear to be more than simply the existence of channels for communication. What is specially notable about the dialogue around environmental issues is that it is frequently conducted in a climate of charges and counter charges of irrationality, with each side exasperated at the apparent failure of the other to grasp the argument and to see reason.

'One can understand and to some extent sympathise with the prevalent near-puritanical reaction to the rapid technology-based economic growth of the post-war world. But to see the reason for it and to sympathise with the attitudes behind it, is not the same thing as agreeing that it is a rational and sound reaction. It is, on the contrary, a largely irrational reaction stemming from deep emotional conviction rather than any dispassionate analysis of the problems and the practical options for dealing with them' (Brookes 1976).

This example is typical of many. In his Dimbleby lecture (*Listener* 1978), Lord Rothschild referred to environmentalists as 'eco-maniacs' and 'eco-nuts'. And in a lecture to an American conference reported in *The Times* (12.10.78), Paul Johnson similarly referred to the ecological lobby as 'simply irrational; but irrationality is an enemy of civilised society, and can be, and is, exploited by the politically interested'. On the other side of the debate, *The Ecologist* (Spring 1978) concluded from its review of the Windscale Inquiry that 'reason and truth no longer prevail at Public Inquiries.' It is not surprising that the statement concluded that the only course open is a programme of non-violent disobedience. Some would go further: it is the rationality of modern societies, dominated by the values of 'technology–organisation–efficiency–growth–progress . . .' whose sanity is called into question:

'. . . only such single valued mindlessness would cut down the last redwood, pollute the most beautiful beaches, invent machines to injure and destroy plant and human life. To have only one value, is, in human terms, to be mad. It is to be a machine' (Reich 1971).

The 'irrational' character of the debate is generally diagnosed as being due to a failure to settle crucial scientific and technical issues. Opposition to nuclear energy is seen to be irrational, because the scientific evidence demonstrates it to be safer than windmills (Rothschild 1978; Inhaber n.d.). A more sophisticated version recognizes that the evidence of those who have an interest in an issue may be partial or distorted. So, it is argued, the way to ensure a rational debate for the inquiry on fast-breeder reactors is to set up more broad-based machinery which would not be dependent on those institutionally committed to official options, but would be able to initiate, conduct or commission independent research (Baker 1979). In short, the problem of achieving rationality is seen to be fundamentally one of getting the facts right, and of discovering the right technical and organizational solutions.

Such an approach is too simplistic. In the first place, 'getting the facts right' is frequently more complex than the technocratic mode of reasoning recognizes. In making a judgement on the reliability of data, we take account of its source. And here, environmentalists frequently differ. They do not share the confidence of many in the advice of experts, and are particularly cautious when those experts are employed by the protagonists in the debate. They are likely to point out too that experts disagree, and can muster supporters with acceptable credentials whom they believe to be closer to the truth. Moreover, expert opinion itself undergoes change. Fresh evidence comes to light which undermines confidence. Take, for example, changes in expert opinion on levels of radiation which are hazardous. Firstly, these have steadily been adjusted downwards. At one time it was believed that radiation was hazardous only beyond a certain threshold. It is now generally accepted that the relation between radiation and hazard is a linear one, so that each dose, however small, increases the risk of morbidity. Secondly, there is disagreement among experts on the effects of various levels.

At the more mundane level, action typically has to go beyond rigorously established experimental evidence, as every engineer knows. Calculations take us so far, but on many issues not far enough. Steam engines worked long before scientists had solved all the problems of thermodynamics. In short, the cognitive basis for action is far more complex than that implied by the technocratic mode. And it is this that lies behind the environmentalists' sometimes articulate and sometimes more intuitive reservations or even hostility towards the technocratic mode of reasoning, which often assumes with disarming simplicity that it is all a question of getting the facts right.

But, as we argued in Chapter 2, the problems of political communication go deeper than this. Facts are interpreted and acquire meaning within the framework of broader systems of beliefs and values—*paradigms*. The existence of alternative social paradigms may result in problems of communication and understanding of such magnitude that they threaten the legitimacy of the political system. It is because protagonists to the debate approach issues from different cultural contexts, which generate different and conflicting implicit meanings, that there is mutual exasperation and charges and counter charges of irrationality and unreason. What is sensible from one point of view is nonsense from another. It is the implicit, self-evident, taken-for-granted character of paradigms which clogs the channels of communication. And, where belief in the reasonableness of the political system, and its openness to reasoned argument and debate, break down, the normal channels of petition, protest, and pressure group tactics come to be seen as inadequate.

The debate on nuclear energy provides an illustration.[8] The sixth report of the standing Royal Commission on Environmental Pollution (Chairman Sir Brian Flowers) was devoted to *Nuclear Power and the Environment* (Cmnd.6118 1976). In its deliberations it explored not only the scientific and technical issues of radiation, the technology of nuclear power, reactor safety and waste management, but also the social, political and ethical issues involved. The main thrust of the report can be summarized:

'We have explained our reasons for thinking that nuclear development raises long-term issues of unusual range and difficulty which are political and ethical, as well as technical in character. We regard the future implications of the plutonium economy as so serious that we should not wish to become committed to this cause unless it is clear that the issues have been fully appreciated and weighed: in view of their nature we believe this can be assured only in the light of wide public understanding. We are perfectly clear that there has so far been very little official consideration of these matters. The view that was expressed by the Department of Energy in their evidence to us was that there were reasonable prospects that the safety and environmental problems posed by nuclear power could be satisfactorily overcome and that, if this proved not to be so, other forms of energy would have to be used, or consumption somehow reduced. We see this as a policy that could lead to the recognition of the dangers when it would be too late to avoid them. More is needed here than bland, unsubstantiated official assurance that the environmental impact of nuclear power has been taken fully into account' (Flowers 1976, para.521).

'. . . There is a need, we believe, openly and deliberately to weigh the risks and costs of embarking on a major nuclear programme against those of not doing so' (Flowers 1976, para.522).

'. . . The ultimate aim is clear; it is to enable decisions on major questions of nuclear development to take place by explicit political process . . . .' (Flowers 1976, para.524).

Their conclusion that there should be no commitment to a large nuclear programme without full public and political debate rested on a very wide-ranging exploration of the economic, social and political issues. These include grave concern about the more long-term security issues, nuclear proliferation, and environmental effects on climate. They were not convinced about official estimates on the link between increased economic activity and energy use and projections of future energy demands, and were concerned that the cost and momentum of the technological development of nuclear energy would preempt the consideration of alternative sources.

The Windscale Inquiry (Report by the Hon. Mr. Justice Parker 1978) was remarkable for its contrast with the Flowers Report. Such differences flowed in part from its restricted terms of reference—to enquire into the reprocessing of nuclear waste. It concluded that in the light of dwindling supplies of fossil fuel, there is no alternative to substituting other sources or converting to a low-energy life style which will not be acceptable to the vast majority. Alternative sources and conservation are recognized to be important,

'but to divert available resources to such efforts to an extent which would prejudice a large scale reliance on nuclear power should it be needed would . . . be an act of bad management'.

On waste management, Mr. Justice Parker considered success could be confidently predicted. On radiation hazards, Parker finds it difficult to believe that there are any members of the public so lacking in generosity that they would refuse to accept the risk for some demonstrable benefit. On proliferation, the Report concluded that THORP would not add to existing risks, which would not in any case arise for at least ten years. On civil liberties, Mr. Parker admitted that he could see no solution beyond requiring that the Government should ensure that interference goes no further than our protection demands. The terrorist threat he considers could be safeguarded by the technical solution of irradiating fuel rods.

It can be seen that whereas the Flowers Report challenges and questions official governmental viewpoints, and is indeed outspokenly critical on some issues, the Parker Report comes down in support of the official line, both that of government departments and of the nuclear industry. Whereas the Flowers Report recognized the ethical and political issues and the profound social implications of nuclear power the Parker Report confined itself largely to technical and organizational considerations. The reaction of the environmentalists can be exemplified by the *Ecologist*'s reply, entitled significantly, 'Reprocessing the Truth':

'At issue with the Inquiry was the future shape of our society and a number of objectors argued that if mankind is to survive, an alternative must be found to our present high energy, growth oriented lifestyle. Parker listened to them but *gave them no* credence (our italics). He accepts the status quo of our industrial society without question, arguing that only nuclear energy can give us the power to progress.'

What the Parker Report did was to interpret the evidence in the light of the dominant social paradigm. And in so doing meaningful dialogue and communication was distorted. Moreover as the environmentalists point out, it confounded technical with political issues. On radiation, for example,

'Parker accepts that any radiation over and above that from natural sources must do biological harm. The question is not therefore a purely scientific one, but a moral one: *how many extra cases of cancer and congenital diseases are a just price to pay for the extra fuel that THORP will put at our disposal and for the extra money it will earn for us to be reprocessing Japanese wastes*' (*Ecologist* 1978, para.2.4).

It is precisely such ethical issues which the Flowers Report recognized must be matters for political debate.

It is important to identify and distinguish beliefs from values in this account. The pro-nuclear lobby both believes that nuclear power will generate economic benefits and that these are desirable. A study in Austria (Otway *et al.* 1978) makes this point more clearly, and argues that 'attitudes' are the way in which beliefs and feelings combine. So a favourable attitude to nuclear power would require both the belief that it will raise the standard of living and a feeling that this is a good thing. Put very simply, beliefs × values = attitudes. Otway and his associates then distinguish between four main clusters of attributes:

1. *Psychological risk factor* (e.g. exposing myself to risk without my consent, and exposing myself to risks which I cannot control).
2. *Economic and technical benefits factor* (e.g. raising the standard of living and provide good economic value).
3. *Socio-political risk factor* (e.g. leading to rigorous physical security measures, and leading to dependency on small groups of highly trained specialized experts).
4. *Environmental and physical risk factor* (e.g. leading to water pollution, leading to long-term modification of the climate).

Where the antagonists differ was not so much in their beliefs about, for example, environmental and physical risks, but in the importance which they attach to various dimensions. For those in favour, it was the economic benefits which contributed most to their attitudes: for those against, it was the importance of risk, both socio-political and psychological, which most explained their attitude. The evidence points to the same conclusion — that support for or opposition to nuclear power is far more than a technical question of risk: its meaning and significance is buried in opposing systems of beliefs and values. And as we will argue later, such systems also serve to justify and legitimate policies — that is, they function as ideologies. Technical questions are then inextricably embedded in ideologies, since they are always related to human intentions and interests.

The debate on nuclear power goes far beyond technical questions: its acceptability or rejection cannot be separated from larger clusters of beliefs and values, which ultimately give the use or rejection of nuclear power meaning and significance.[9] The point can be further reinforced by evidence from an analysis of testimony to the U.S. Congressional Joint Committee on Atomic Energy, which demonstrates forcefully that the debate is rooted in 'ideological cleavages'[10] (Del Sesto 1980). The arguments on both sides can be shown to constitute coherent and antagonistic systems of beliefs and values. The pro-nuclear paradigm stresses the economic benefits (raising the standard of living, and increasing economic growth) and its contribution to the energy crisis (as a source of unlimited energy). It also professes faith in science and technology to solve both the practical problems and the associated political and value issues. By contrast, the anti-nuclear paradigm stresses the legacy to future generations: that it will lead to a totalitarian state, will result in restrictions on individual freedom, proliferation and eventual war. It also rejects the view that science and technology can solve the problems. A second main theme in the anti-nuclear paradigm is related to political accountability and decentralization: that political decision-making should be decentralized, and more responsive.

VALUES FOR MONEY: FLOWERS OR PRODUCTION?

Paradigms then are not only cognitive maps: they also include values — beliefs about what is important. And these generate special problems of communication — even when it is recognized that they are at the heart of the matter (Ashby 1978). Moral discourse presents particular difficulties for the scientific perspective. Judgements of morality are never simply matters of fact, however relevant facts may be. An 'ought' statement always goes beyond an 'is' statement. So this makes moral argument especially difficult to prove. No cool detached analysis of observable facts or testing hypotheses will settle the argument for those who prefer the Beatles to Beethoven. Yet it is competing and conflicting values which are at the centre of many environmental controversies. Environmentalists really do feel strongly about the kind of society which pollutes rivers, and which they would argue plays Russian roulette with nuclear reactors. The pejorative epithets of their opponents who refer to them as 'mobs on the streets' may be understandable. But they too are giving vent to an equally emotional commitment to a different scale of values. What is at stake in short is not just the pollution of a river, or the lives of some seals, but, as we have seen, conflicting views of the moral and social order. It is a conflict of values which is central to the debate.[11]

The inclusion of values in the equation may also raise difficulties for scientists and technologists. In their daily activities, they are above all preoccupied with the discovery of the best means to achieve an end: that is, their concerns are with *instrumental or technical rationality*. Indeed, one finds more than a hint that they are not too well disposed to the messy business of politics, caught up in hunches, intuitions and judgements. There is a tendency to see even this sphere as one where the goals or values are relatively unproblematic, and which would be greatly improved by a healthy injection of numeracy and rigorous logic. Of course, there are times when the scientist or technologist has moral doubts about the objects of his activity. But by and large they are likely to accept the view that the rationale for science and technology is its contribution to economic growth, the creation of wealth, and a rising standard of living—especially if they have chosen to work in productive industry.

The debate over the Cow Green reservoir will serve to exemplify the problem of values. A proposal to build a reservoir in Upper Teesdale met with objections on the grounds that it threatened the survival of what many botanists considered a unique community of rare plants (glacial relict flora). The debate turned on the question of weighing the benefits of preserving the flowers against the economic costs of the loss of employment and export markets if the reservoir were not built. Lord Leatherland put the issue nicely:

'In my own simple way I am asking whether I should decide between flowers on the one hand, and people on the other—people and their prosperity . . . I come down solidly against flowers' (Quoted in Gregory 1971).

It may look simple to the noble lord. But it is not. The crux of the problem centres on the translation of one scale of values to another: economic values against non-economic values. There is no difficulty in translating degrees Centigrade into degrees Fahrenheit. All you need to know is the 'conversion' factor, or the relative value of one degree versus another. The two scales are commensurable and can be interchanged. Proponents of cost–benefit analysis are trying to do the same thing. They say, if we can calculate the extra cost of finding an alternative site and then ask if people are prepared to pay that much for the preservation of the flowers, then we can come to a rational decision. But some scales of values are not commensurable. You cannot translate degrees centigrade into cubic centimetres. They are different values: one is temperature and the other cubic capacity. This can be put dramatically in calculations of the value of human life. Economists have approached this in a number of ways, for example, by capitalizing the loss of earnings. At first sight, the approach seems sensible enough. But put the issue differently: ask a wife—how much would you sell your husband for, or your child? If everything has a price, and can be reduced to an economic calculus, then such a question would not shock. What exasperates the environmentalists is that the value which provides the criterion is not one which they can accept.

Cost–benefit analysis takes for granted that economic values and criteria provide the ultimate arbiter; that any action is justified if it pays, and is not justifiable if the economic costs are too high. Now not even the most enthusiastic defender of the market is prepared to go quite as far as that and to admit free trade in children or pornography. There are some circumstances in which higher order values override the imperatives of the market place, and into which cost is not allowed to enter. The environmentalists seeking to save the flowers are saying just this. But the supporters of the reservoir take it for granted as common sense that economic criteria are more important, and that if it is a choice between flowers or production, then the flowers must go.

Disputes over amenities then are essentially political. They involve a clash of values. And these are properly resolved by the political system. The technocratic mode operates below this level within the framework of agreed political values and seeks to depoliticize such issues by reducing them to an economic calculus. For many, amenity (beauty or scientific truth) cannot be quantified. Where some hold strongly to values which they see to be higher order values and these are not part of the taken-for-granted values of the technocratic consciousness, there is exasperation and emotion — on both sides — rooted in fundamental failures of understanding. The predominant scientific/technical rationality of modern industrial societies simply finds it difficult to come to grips with differences in values. There is really no vocabulary, no style of thinking within the dominant culture which resolves the flower versus production value conflict. On the contrary, the dominant technocratic mode dismisses such arguments as coloured by ill-informed sentiment, and therefore irrational. Even where it is recognized that these are conflicts of values there is difficulty in accepting these as a basis for rational decisions. Rationality is defined in such a way that it is reduced to an economic calculus. So, for example, in a scrupulously fair analysis of the Cow Green Reservoir debate, Roy Gregory concludes that those who took part in the debate reacted in predictable ways:

'spontaneously and instinctively, and by reason of their background and interests, their hearts were on one side or the other. . . . To judge from their speeches, several peers . . . had adopted a more rational and open-minded attitude, asking themselves what really would be the cost to industry . . ., and . . . the cost to scientific research' (Gregory 1971 p.190).

So, for Roy Gregory too, it is careful weighing of costs, not strong sentiments for scientific research or the beauty of the countryside which characterizes a rational decision. Yet it would be equally rational to come to the decision using criteria derived from the pursuit of a non-economic goal. There is no self-evident *a priori* reason why one value should be *the* criterion of rationality.

Values are not rational. But this is not the same thing as saying that they are irrational. To refer to values as sentiments or emotions is to demote them. It is characteristic of the technocratic mode to treat them in this way. The crux of the problem is that in industrial societies material values predominate. This ensures a built-in bias in the operation of the political process. The issue was succinctly put in a closing speech in the House of Lords debate:

'Lord Strang conceded that in the circumstances the Committee probably could not have come to any other conclusion. There was a lesson to be learned from this case, and they ought to be clear what the moral was. A body of presuppositions governed the development of modern society. . . . When conflicts like Cow Green occurred, these presuppositions served almost universally to resolve the conflict in one way rather than another. . . . They had been spelt out by J. K. Galbraith in the last of his Reith Lectures for 1966. There he had outlined what he took to be the faith of modern industrial man, the goals and values which determine his conduct, to which everyone . . . was expected to give priority. These were: technology is always good: accordingly firms must always expand; the consumption of goods is the principle source of happiness; idleness is wicked as an alternative to work, and finally, nothing should interfere with the priority that we accord to technology, growth, and increased consumption' (Gregory 1971).

It is in this way that the industrial system continues to have a monopoly of social purpose.

PARADIGMS, IDEOLOGIES, AND LEGITIMACY

Paradigms are not only beliefs about what the world is like and guides to action: they also serve the function of legitimating or justifying courses of action. That is to say, they function as ideologies. Those who do not share the paradigm will question the justification for the action it supports. Hence, conflicts over what constitutes the paradigm by which action should be guided and judged to be reasonable is itself a part of the political process.[12] The struggle to universalize a paradigm is part of the struggle for power. Parties to a conflict will draw on all the resources they can muster, and will raid the cultural repertoire for beliefs and values which will authorize and provide acceptable reasons for their actions and support their interests. Each will seek to impose their own definitions on the other. Failure to get the others to see reason—that is to accept their rationality—can also explain the sense of frustration and anger which exemplifies the debate. It is precisely because the beliefs are so politically important in conferring legitimacy, and thus reinforcing power and influence, that they become the centre of acrimonious debate. Hence the emotion with which many attack the environmentalists.

Our hypothesis is then that support for various forms of outsider political structures and processes will be most marked for those who do not share the dominant social paradigm within which these operate. As we expect, support for direct action turns out to be significantly more marked among environmentalists than industrialists: 64% of environmentalists would support direct action to influence government decisions on environmental issues, compared with 60% of the industrialists who oppose such action (Table 5.4). The hypothesis gains further support from analysis of the general public. Moreover, support for direct action is directly related to indices of commitment to or rejection of the dominant social paradigm. It varies directly with scores on both the post-material values scale and on the economic individualism scale (Table 5.5).[13]

Table 5.4. Support for direct action

Direct action	Environmentalists		Public		Industrialists	
	N	%	N	%	N	%
Strongly support	81	19.4	20	7.4	6	3.0
Support	187	44.8	84	31.2	41	20.3
Undecided	85	20.4	89	33.1	34	16.8
Not support	56	13.4	63	23.4	75	37.1
Strongly opposed	8	1.9	13	4.8	46	22.8

Table 5.5. Support for direct action by support for economic individualism*

Direct action	Environmentalists			Public			Industrialists		
	Mean	S.D.	N	Mean	S.D.	N	Mean	S.D.	N
Strongly support	29.1	14.9	75	48.4	9.3	17	70.4	10.5	6
Support	37.7	14.2	178	51.4	14.1	75	62.9	13.8	41
Undecided	45.6	14.3	81	56.7	11.1	80	64.9	12.8	33
Not support	48.0	12.9	55	58.2	11.0	58	65.7	12.8	73
Strongly opposed	59.5	13.5	7	64.3	17.0	11	71.2	11.8	46

*Scale score (%)

ENVIRONMENTALISM, CLASS, AND PARTY

So, we can understand why environmentalists lack confidence in political processes. They do not share the dominant social paradigm, which persistently legitimates and justifies courses of action which they oppose. And the channels of political communication are clogged by incomprehension. Hence the resort to direct action. But we are not suggesting that this is the only or complete explanation. Political parties are another major channel for feeding demands into the political system. They occupy the boundary between society and government. Parties seek to aggregate a wide range of interests into coherent policies in order to maximize support. It is possible that the resort to outsider politics is at least in part related to the more general loss of confidence in political parties. But there may be other reasons. It is understandable that the traditional environmentalists should adopt pressure group tactics around single issues. But the new radical environmentalists are concerned not simply with single issues such as the protection of birds and whales, pollution, and the exhaustion of non-renewable resources. They seek more wide-ranging and fundamental social changes. And so do the trade union officials, though they, unlike the radical environmentalists, are prepared to work through political parties. In short, the political expression of environmentalism raises further questions about the working of the political system.

Pressure groups concerned with single issues usually seek to avoid partisan political alignments. The protection of wildlife, for example, can be seen to cut across traditional party cleavages. Some environmentalists too see environmental protection as a matter of public interest rising above class and party. Others wish to adopt meliorist strategies relying on consciousness-raising activities to bring about the necessary changes in the hearts and minds of individuals. But in order to achieve any substantial impact some will feel that it is necessary to exercise a more direct influence on the political system. Hence direct action.

The alternative of working through the party system involves seeking alliances and coalitions of interests. One way is to attempt to influence the policies of the major parties as directly as possible by means of a dialogue with those who are sympathetic and influential within the parties. This is the strategy of the Green Alliance in Britain. But whatever method adopted of seeking alliances and coalitions, there are obvious difficulties. In their political affiliations 46% of the new environmentalists identify with the left, compared with 68% of trade union officials, and only 8% of nature conservationists (Table 5.6). But it must not be overlooked that 37% of environmentalists

Table 5.6. Political affiliations

	Indust-rialists %	Trade Unionists %	Environ-mentalists %	Nature Conserva-tionists %	Public %
Left	1.4	24.8	15.3	0.7	7.2
Mildly left	7.2	42.0	30.5	7.1	16.2
Centre	16.9	17.5	19.9	24.2	25.8
Mildly right	47.3	8.0	13.7	34.5	16.6
Right	21.3	2.6	3.8	25.3	10.7
No position	5.8	5.1	16.8	8.2	23.6
	100.0	100.0	100.0	100.0	100.0
$N =$	(207)	(274)	(417)	(281)	(458)

classified themselves as either 'centre' or 'no position'. One of the bases for the emergence of 'green' or ecology parties is the conviction that the traditional left/right dimension in politics has little relevance to environmental issues. Parties of the left are seen to be as committed to economic goals as are those of the right, differing mainly in their support for economic individualism versus varying degrees of collectivism.

But the left also attaches importance to non-economic goals including welfare. Indeed, the rise of social democracy at the end of the nineteenth century gave cultural and political expression to opposition to the cruder manifestations of economic liberalism (Chapter 4). What the 'new' politics brings to the surface and feeds in to the political system are demands stemming from non-economic values. But these have always constituted an element in left wing politics, which has never lent support to unbridled economism, and whose dream of a new Jerusalem has gone beyond material goals, however important these have been for those suffering material deprivation and inequality.[14] There is no doubt about the polarization between the dominant business culture and the new left, as this is expressed in radical environmentalism. But such an emphasis neglects the extent to which the old left encapsulates an alternative culture, which may provide a bridge between the business culture and the 'adversary' culture.

The point can be put more explicitly by looking at the evidence from our sample of trade union officials. What is especially interesting is the way in which they bridge the crucial differences in values between environmentalists and industrialists in the sense that they give high priority to *both* material *and* non-material values. They share the importance attached to economic goals by industrialists. But like the environmentalists, they too give high priority to non-economic goals and values. In short, trade union officials reject a crucial element in the dominant social paradigm — the simple hegemony of economic values. They, like the environmentalists, see the need for the public interest to override market mechanisms, emphasize participation against authority, and collective provision of welfare and the reassertion of community. Indeed, on most issues, they polarize more strongly than environmentalists: their ideal society is even more radically opposed. They differ too in their confidence in science and technology.

So, we can revise our map of competing paradigms to include the old or traditional left, as exemplified by our sample of trade union officials (Figure 5.1). It would seem that radical environmentalists come close to the traditional left on a number of dimensions. But there remain crucial differences. Although we have little direct evidence, we suspect that the way in which nature is valued, and man's relations with nature as perceived by the traditional left may be closer to the dominant paradigm. On the crucial issue of the overriding importance of economic goals and criteria, the traditional left at least shares with the new environmentalits a commitment to non-economic values. But it differs in supporting economic growth which environmentalists actively oppose.

Of course, it is necessary to be cautious in drawing conclusions about the left, or about rank and file trade union members from a sample of branch officials. Although these constitute an important influence in politics, we cannot conclude that trade union policies closely reflect the views of officials. Indeed, a much smaller proportion of members than officials are left in politics (*Sunday Times* 31/8/80). Nevertheless, trade unions are particularly concerned with a range of environmental issues which overlap particularly with those of the new environmentalists. As we saw in Chapter 1, officials consider noise and toxic waste to be particularly urgent problems. And trade union policies have shown especial concern in recent years with the working environment, focusing especially on safety. In the U.S.A., it is necessary to distinguish between two types of union (Logan and Nelkin 1980). Firstly there

	DOMINANT PARADIGM	TRADITIONAL LEFT	NEW ENVIRONMENTAL PARADIGM
CORE VALUES	Material (economic) goals Natural environment valued as resource Domination over nature	Material *and* non-material goals ? ?	Non-material (self-actualization) Natural environment intrinsically valued Harmony with nature
ECONOMY	Market forces Risk and reward Rewards for achievement Differentials Individual self-help	Public interest Safety Other criteria Egalitarian? Collective/social provision	Public interest Safety Other criteria Egalitarian Collective/social provision
POLITY	Authoritative structures: (experts influential) Hierarchical More law and order	Participative structures Non-hierarchical Less law and order	Participative structures: (citizen/worker involvement) Non-hierarchical Less law and order
NATURE	Ample reserves Nature hostile/neutral Environment controllable	Some shortages ? ?	Earth's resources limited Nature benign Nature delicately balanced
KNOWLEDGE	Confidence in science and technology	Confidence in science: reservations re technology	Limits to science: appropriate technology

Figure 5.1 Alternative paradigms

are the 'business' unions whose main function is to mediate between members and employers to maximize the wage effort bargain. Secondly, there are what Nelkin labels the 'service' unions, whose policies are shaped by broader political values and objectives. It is these latter unions in particular who have shown concern for environmental impact.

What this evidence does is to point to the difficulties facing environmentalists in seeking alliances within the party system. On political and social issues, they have more in common with the left. In their shared concern with traditional environmentalists over issues such as pollution and the threat to endangered species, their allies are generally antagonistic to their political ideology. So they find themselves in an ambiguous relation with traditional parties. Nuclear power faces the traditional party system with similar difficulties. Parties of both left and right include both protagonists and opposers (Nelkin and Pollak 1980b). The virtual exclusion of nuclear power from party politics leaves little alternative to the protesters but various forms of 'outsider' politics.

A NEW MIDDLE CLASS?

A more fundamental objection to coalitions between environmentalists and the left derives from locating them as 'middle class', so that their interests diverge from or are in conflict with those of the working class. Judged by criteria such as income, education and occupation, environmentalists have been widely labelled 'middle class'. But this is too simple. It fails to come to grips with the facts that the most outspoken antagonism to the environmentalist movement in recent years has come from affluent and well-educated industrialists who would also be described as middle class. To locate environmentalists as middle class therefore has little explanatory value.

The problem of identifying the precise class location of environmentalists raises complex definitional and theoretical problems. Firstly, the concept of 'middle class' is of doubtful value for sociological analysis. It is certainly possible to identify those occupations which are labelled middle class by significant sections of the population. But the occupations so identified vary according to the social location of individuals. And so do the criteria. Labelling an individual as middle or working class appears to have little more significance than the conferment of social status.[15] And this will depend on what are the valued criteria. For some this is income; for others it is behaviour, including the achievement of honorific symbols such as education, dress, speech and manners, or performing some valued role in society.

Analyses of class in industrial societies, especially those in the Marxist tradition, have been overwhelmingly preoccupied with the way in which the capitalist relations of production generate antagonisms and conflicts of interest within societies in which the production of goods and services for sale is the dominant activity. Such a model has faced considerable difficulty in relating a 'middle' class of managers, technicians, and service workers, to the two main antagonistic classes. What is notable is the almost complete omission of any extended discussion of the particular fraction of the middle class which has been identified in this analysis: those operating in those sub-systems in industrial societies concerned with the pursuit of non-economic values, and functioning outside the market, and in this sense, non-capitalistic elements persisting within capitalist societies (Crompton and Gubbay 1977, pp.81–85). Many theorists in the Marxist tradition see the 'new middle class' as playing an essentially subaltern role as servants of power. Poulantzas (1975), for example considers their ideology to be rooted in their lack of real power: any specific bourgeois radicalism taking the form of anarcho-syndicalism. Others have emphasized the structural ambiguity of members of an intermediary class between capital and labour, who are volatile and politically unstable in their loyalties (Crompton and Gubbay 1977, pp.174–175, 196–203).[16]

One solution is to seek to assimilate these groups into what are seen to be the two main contending classes. So, for example, the most senior scientific and technical positions can be located as members of the ruling class, or as servants of power, while the lower ranks of wage earners are seen to be steadily de-skilled and proletarianized (Braverman 1974). According to one variation of this view, teachers, social workers, and intellectuals who contribute to the 'hegemony of bourgeois ideology' are part of the bourgeois class, while those who contribute to the ideology of the proletariat are part of the working class (Gramsci 1971). A variation of this view is put forward by Poulantzas who argues that intellectuals should be excluded from the working class because they are unproductive. Since they share the essential elements of petty bourgeois ideology, he argues that they are properly located as a part of this class (Wright 1979).

An alternative approach starts from a distinction between the functions of an intermediary group of intellectuals and experts and their structural location as employees. It argues that although their function is to contribute to the reproduction of labour, and thus to serve the interests of the bourgeoisie, their structural position as employees locates them outside the bourgeoisie. From this it is argued that they occupy a contradictory location within class relations, rooted in their position of structural ambiguity. Unlike other wage labour, teachers and social workers have a measure of control over their own labour and can be described as semi-autonomous. Yet like workers, they must sell their labour power in order to live. They occupy a contradictory location in the sense that they share interests with both the working class and the petty bourgeoisie (Wright 1979).

A third approach argues for the emergence of a new class, with identifi-able interests, and occupying a location distinct from bourgeoisie, petty bourgeoisie, or proletariat. Gouldner (1979), for example, sees the new class as internally divided between a technical intelligentsia and humanistic intellectuals. B. and J. Ehrenreich identify a new professional-management class 'who do not own the means of production and whose major function in the social division of labour may be described broadly as the reproduction of capitalist culture and capitalist class relations' (Walker 1979, p.12). The relations between the professional–managerial and the working class are essentially those of control and subordination: that is, they are antagonistic. But the professional–management class are also antagonistic to the capitalist class. They are constantly seeking to assert their autonomy against the bourgeoisie: *vide* the perennial struggles over academic freedom and the attempts of universities to carve out an independent role, and not simply to accept the subordinate role of meeting the needs of industry.

The complexity of the debate is of necessity oversimplified. Nor can it be resolved here. But our data are highly relevant to advancing an understanding of the issues. One of the difficulties with the debate is that it is mostly highly theoretical: there is little attempt at a rigorous empirical test of alternative viewpoints.[17] Our own data point to some tentative conclusions on the class location of environmentalists. At the level of ideology, the majority reject the ideology of market capitalism. How this affects their behaviour we cannot say. But it is hardly plausible to accept them as passive instruments in 'the ideological state apparatus'. Potentially, at least, many of them are more likely to adopt a critical role as social workers, teachers, or writers. Secondly, their ideology appears to share much with that of the working class left as exemplified by trade union officials. But their relative autonomy as employees, combined with their authority in relation to most working class roles, leads them to be more ambivalent towards authority, and less committed to participative structures. Their second main difference is in their lack of commitment to material and economic goals compared with the traditional left. Unlike the trade union officials, environmentalists share the dominant paradigm view that material and non-material values are antagonistic. But they plump for non-material goals and values. Again, this can be seen as fundamentally related to their social role: an everyday occupational commitment to non-material goals and values.

In short, we have identified a group of individuals with a distinctive ideology which is understandable in terms of their social relations, and their relation to the productive processes (Figure 5.2). Our analysis suggests that environmentalism is an expression of the interests of those whose class position in the 'non-productive' sector locates them at the periphery of the institutions and processes of industrial capitalist societies. Hence their concern to win greater participation and influence and thus to strengthen the political role of their members. It is a protest against alienation from the processes of decision making, and the depoliticization of issues through the usurpation of policy decisions by experts, operating within the dominant economic values. It is the political dimensions of their role which goes far to account for their particular form of dissent.

But this is only part of the answer. Their attack is not simply rooted in their subordinate position. It is also a challenge to the goals and values of the dominant class, and the structures and institutions through which these are realized. Environmentalists' rejection of beliefs in the efficacy of the market, risk-taking and reward for achievement, and of the overriding goal of economic growth and of economic criteria is a challenge to the hegemonic ideology which legitimates the institutions and politics of industrial capitalism. Central to the operation of such societies is the role of the market. It is the relation between individuals and those sub-systems of society which operate either within or largely outside the market which we will argue is the clue to the clash of value systems and social paradigms.

	DOMINANT	SUBORDINATE	AUTONOMOUS
MARKET	a. Dominant (hegemonic) class: owners, managers b. Servants of power: technocrats, bureaucrats	Proletariat: clerical/manual workers in market sector	a. Petite bourgeoisie principles/owners small business b. Business professions; accountants, architects
NON-MARKET	Intellectual establishment e.g. heads of public (non-productive) corporations	Clerical and other workers in non-market sector (local government)	a. Personal service professions; (doctors) and Semi professions: (health, education, welfare) b. Creative arts/intellectuals

Figure 5.2. Dimensions of class interest

What we are suggesting then is that any understanding of the quite different values and beliefs of environmentalists and industrialists is to be found in part in their relations to the core economic institutions of society. Environmentalists are drawn predominantly from a specific fraction of the middle class whose interests and values diverge markedly from other groups in industrial societies.[18] Whether they constitute a distinct class or not is a matter of definition. To define class in terms of some objective criteria such as relation to the means of production, or function, runs the danger of imposing categories which fail to mesh with the consciousness and behaviour of groups of individuals. But if we anchor our discussion in the observable behaviours and utterances of identifiable groups, then there is a strong case for arguing for the emergence of a new class from the 1960s onwards. The growth of a new radicalism among social workers, teachers, lawyers, psychiatrists, sharpened the antagonism between those closely tied to production functions as managers, technologists and scientists, and those in the non-productive welfare and creative occupations. It is the same constituency which has supported the radical environmentalist movement. But the New Left is split. The radicals-in-the-professions have agonized over the interface between the professional–expert and the working class, and have sought to discover ways of eliminating authority relationships between social workers and client, teacher and pupil, doctor and patient. Others have reverted to a more traditional communist analysis, defining issues in terms of economic self-interest, and have shelved any consideration of the historic conflict between managers and workers rooted in the division of labour (Ehrenreichs 1979 p.41). We would wish to stress that the interests, values, and ideology of this particular fraction of the middle class differ from other sections of what can be described as an intellectual class or technocracy. Our sample of indust-rialists included senior engineers. We have been able to aggregate these with senior businessmen precisely because the engineers did not differ on any of the significant variables. They share with the business sample strong support for material values and for the dominant social paradigm. Our conclusions therefore come close to Gouldner's (1979), who sees the new class as internally divided between a (technical) intelligentsia and (humanistic) intellectuals. However, if by class we refer to groups grounded in common economic interests, then it is misleading to refer to these as members of a divided class: we would argue that we have identified antagonistic classes, and that the engineers in our sample would be more accurately described as servants of power, strongly aligned with the economic interests of the market sector.

The central question raised by this analysis is the extent of any relative autonomy of such sub-systems within the framework of the dominant institutions of industrial capitalism. The Marxist tradition sees the institutions of health and welfare as functionally necessary for the reproduction of labour, thus serving the interests of a captalist class. Now while this may possibly explain state support for 'non-productive' sectors, such an explanation does not offer a satisfactory account of either the interests or the values of those who work in the personal service, intellectual, and artistic sectors. Our evidence demonstrates that many such hold values and beliefs which are sharply antagonistic to the dominant ideology.

A CRISIS OF POLITICS?

Almond and Verba's study traced the high level of confidence in political institutions to the effectiveness of participation. Their evidence demonstrated high levels of civic competence; that citizens felt the political system to be both accessible and responsive. Two decades later, the picture is very different. The growth of protest outside the normal channels, and of direct action, all point to a deep-seated loss of confidence in political institutions.

The political significance of the radical environmentalist movement is that it exemplifies some of the challenges facing the political systems of advanced industrial societies. Almond and Verba argued that it is participation through the various channels of political communication which ensures the responsiveness of the system to competing demands. And it is this which guarantees continuing confidence. But the evidence of this study shows that it is precisely here that radical environmentalists face severe difficulties. Because of its taken-for-granted character, the dominant social paradigm can systematically repress the articulation of alternative viewpoints. Given support for economic values and growth, confidence in experts, and in the power of science and technology to come up with answers, then the conclusions of Mr. Justice Parker at Windscale can be seen to be not only reasonable but right. Given the acceptance of the dominant goals and values of society, problems are seen to be essentially questions of means, soluble by harnessing knowledge and expertise to the political process. Rationality is defined in narrowly technical or instrumental terms. What are properly political questions involving conflicts of values and interests are de-politicized and treated as technical questions; what Habermas (1971) refers to as the 'scientisation of politics'. This, it is argued, is precisely what happened at Windscale. It is under such conditions that political institutions distort communications and there is no genuine dialogue. There is little doubt that alternative social paradigms generate major problems of communication and understanding. Hence the charges and counter-charges of unreason and irrationality between environmentalists and supporters of the status quo. The Flowers Report concluded that 'arguments of both sides of the debate deserve to be heard with greater mutual understanding' (p.191). This analysis draws attention to the deep seated problems which are raised by such an apparently reasonable hope.

Environmental problems such as lead in petrol and nuclear power face representative political processes with special difficulties. Because of their technical complexity, they have facilitated the depoliticization of issues and the shift of decisions away from parliaments to inaccessible administrative bureaucracies. Environmental issues exemplify the more general trend towards a widening of the gap between citizen and government, and the growing concentration of state power which it is argued underlies an emerging crisis of legitimacy in politics (Habermas 1976).

Environmentalists face special difficulties in finding a niche within the political party spectrum, especially in countries such as Britain where the electoral system makes it extremely difficult for minority interests to find an independent political expression. Our evidence suggests that radical environmentalists are drawn from a distinct fraction of the 'middle class' whose interests cannot be assimilated into either of what are seen by Marxist analysts as the two main contending classes. Their interests do not coincide with those of manual wage earners though they intersect and overlap. In their opposition to many facets of industrial capitalism, they are more likely to be able to form alliances with the left than the right. But on some issues their interests cut across the traditional left/right dimension. Most important, they differ from the left in their rejection of the importance of economic goals. Their class and party interest place them in an ambiguous position in relation to the major political divisions in industrial societies. It is to the implications of this analysis for the future of industrial societies that we now turn.

NOTES

1. Marsh (1977) distinguishes between five different political styles: conformists, reformists, revolutionaries, activists, and protesters. It is with the reformists and activists that we are mainly concerned. The protesters are a-political; they do not participate in conventional politics. They constitute between 20% (U.S.A.) and 30% (Netherlands). They are more likely to be young, and female, and average or below in education. Though they constitute an important and disturbing element in western politics, this study is focused mainly on conformists, reformists and activists.
2. For a detailed exploration of such differences in Sweden, Holland and Austria, and the way in which they affected the form and expression of protest on environmental and technological issues, see Nelkin 1977.
3. For a critique, see Angus Steward in Crouch 1977, pp.19–37.
4. Bell did not say that all ideological thinking was over though he was widely misinterpreted. Rather, he drew attention to the 'restless search for a new intellectual radicalism' (Bell 1962, pp.374–5).
5. It is not, of course, the only example. Discontent on the right has also generated its own rebels, e.g. the self-employed and ratepayers. Their discontent is rooted in some of the same circumstances, such as opposition to bureaucratization (see King and Nugent 1979).
6. Further evidence of the cynicism with which many view the political system is the finding of a 1972 NOP survey that 67% believe politicians will promise anything to get votes and of an ORC survey in 1973 that 58% consider most politicians are in parliament for what they can get out of it (quoted in Chamberlain 1977 pp.188–189). The surveys also found that a high proportion of the electorate (between 38 and 51%) considers there to be no important differences between the main political parties. Such a view is obviously inconsistent with the ability of the electorate to exercise any real and effective choice between alternative policies (Chamberlain (1977).
7. It could be argued that attitudinal measure are of limited value as indicators of behaviour. It's one thing to agree with a poll question about protecting the environment, but quite another to pay the price. Both our own data and U.S.A. researches (Mitchell 1978) have included questions on trade-offs. We found that a majority put environmental protection before economic growth, but behind employment. The American study found a majority put protection before rising prices.
8. We are indebted to B.Pflemic (1979) for a detailed analysis of the nuclear energy debate and for its valuable insights into its political implications.
9. The Flowers Report recognizes that opposition to nuclear power is rooted in opposition to industrialization. But put this way, it simply neutralizes the issue and explains it away.
10. Ideology is defined here as 'a system of ideas, beliefs and values, which both emotionally steers and cognitively orients individuals and groups of people.' This is close to our use of the concept paradigm. We think it important to maintain a distinction between paradigms and ideologies.

    To define ideology as beliefs distorted by interests runs into the difficulty that it is hard to discover examples where interests cannot be shown to have some influence, however slight.

    Scientific knowledge can be used to legitimate and justify courses of action, and thus become incorporated in an ideology. This approach makes it possible to distinguish between the social factors in the construction of knowledge, including scientific knowledge, and the quite distinct issue of the harnessing of knowledge, including scientific knowledge, to the service of interests (Cotgrove 1978a). For a review of the literature on the social construction of scientific knowledge see Mulkay 1979.

11. Where the importance of values is recognized, it may still be neglected on the grounds that they are slippery things and difficult to measure reliably, or that 'public opinion' is somewhat fickle and is no basis for determining long-term policy. In this way, the values of those in power (which presumably do not change) are protected. See, for example, Warner, in Griffiths 1981 p.xii.

12. We are indebted to Graham Cox for this point. We are not, of course, implying bad faith. The contesters are convinced that the world is as they define it.

13. In a five nation comparison, Inglehart found a similar relationship to hold between support for post-material values, and protest potential (Barnes and Kaase 1979, Chapter 12).

14. The recent rise of the Lucas shop stewards' movement pressing for a shift to socially useful products is an indication of such concerns among trade unionists. See D. Elliott and R. Elliott 1976.

15. This distinction between status and class as economically determined interests derives of course from the work of Max Weber.

16. For an extended discussion and critique of the Marxist approach to class, see Parker 1979.

17. For example, there are constant references to 'objective' class situations. But the terms appears to have a special meaning: that is, it refers to what is real as defined by the theory, by contrast with faulty bourgeois or ideological perceptions. It assumes the acceptance of the Marxist paradigm.

18. We can now see why many previous studies have failed to discover any very clear picture of the social bases of support for environmentalism. Firstly, American studies have generally failed to distinguish between the new radical environmentalist and the conservationist. If we simply relate indices such as politics or occupation to measures of environmental concern we conflate the quite different political and ideological positions of radical and traditional conservationists. Secondly, they have rested on an adequate conceptualization of social class, which has used indices such as income and education, rather than power and relation to the means of production. Denton Morrison and Riley Dunlap (1980), however have drawn attention to the specific occupational locations of environmentalists and the tendency for them to be in occupations which do not have an interest in production.

CHAPTER 6

Alternative Futures

THINKING ABOUT THE FUTURE

This book is not an exercise in futurology, certainly as this enterprise is popularly understood. It is not an attempt to forecast the future. But it *is* a book about the future. It is about the possibilities that the depletion of the earth's resources in fossil fuels and materials may have profound implications for society as we know it. It is about the way society is reacting to this possibility now, and how it might, or could, or have to react in the future. More accurately, it is about the quite different reactions which we find within society.

Thinking about the future is a growth industry. Government agencies, industrial units, and university institutes, writers, the media—all are showing signs of a proliferating activity, rooted in a growing uncertainty and anxiety. And we do not need to look far for the sources of such uncertainty. When environmentalists first began to foretell catastrophe, they were roundly dismissed. Events have to some extent lent credence to their fears, if not to their worst predictions. But more than this, there is also growing evidence of a change of mood: an emerging disenchantment with materialism, and with a scientific and technological world, and a search for some deeper human meaning and significance. Whether such signs are portents of more fundamental long-term changes, it is difficult to say. But the optimistic confidence of the Victorians, and even of a few decades ago, has evaporated. The resultant literature is vast and almost unmanageable.[1] So, to keep our feet on the ground we will take as our point of departure the issues raised by the environmentalist debate.

UTOPIAN THOUGHT AND SOCIAL CHANGE

The general thrust of the new environmentalism is utopian. The term is being used here simply as a convenient label for visions of a better society. The opposite of utopian thought is ideology; beliefs and values which are

101

justifications for the status quo, the preservation of existing institutions and the interests which they serve (Mannheim 1966). Utopias provide scenarios for alternative futures. They imply the possibility of choice. And here we confront perhaps one of the most fundamental issues in thinking about the future. The dominant culture is deterministic. A major mode of thinking about the future is some variant of technological determinism: that machines make history. The industrial revolution, and now the 'new industrial revolution' are terms which imply that technology is the engine which drives the social system. This is nowhere more dramatically illustrated than in the current debate on the electronic revolution. Scarcely a week passes without some media presentation of the way in which microprocessors will transform our lives. Science fiction, similarly, as a genre has typically painted a picture of the future shaped by science. Of course, there has always been an anti-science and anti-machine element, but the exception proves the rule. Trend analysis is from the same stable. It accepts the present and simply extrapolates it into the future (Encel *et al.* 1975).

Utopian thought challenges determinism and presents the possibility of alternative futures. It implies choice. To write utopias off as visionary and unrealizable may itself be an expression of deterministic thinking. But utopian thought raises two main questions. Firstly, is any utopia practical? And secondly, do people want it?

On the second of these questions, there is one fairly firm conclusion. Environmentalists are agreed that there is a lot wrong with contemporary industrial societies, and that fundamental changes are needed. But here, the consensus evaporates. They would generally agree that we need a change in values, and that the dominant material and economic values of industrial society must give way to higher order values. They would also agree about the need for fundamental changes in the structure of society, especially the move towards more small-scale decentralized society, with greater autonomy.[2] But here the conflicts and tensions which bedevil all societies are likely to emerge. It is highly improbable that the readers of *Undercurrents* and the readers of *The Ecologist* or *Vole* would be able to get along happily within the same small-scale, integrated, autonomous village, dedicated to the pursuit of non-material values. Visions of the New Jerusalem have always differed on one important dimension: how to maintain the integration and harmony of the community. Solutions have been variations of two opposing philosophies. One, is the Hobbesian perspective: that order can be achieved only be each surrendering personal freedom to the sovereign. Such philosophies are rooted in an essentially pessimistic view of the nature of man. The alternative springs from a more optimistic view of human nature: that human potentiality for good is thwarted and frustrated by social and political institutions. Given the destruction of repressive political and economic structures, harmony will prevail.

The environmentalist movement is heir to both these traditions. Some of its supporters derive their inspiration from the philosophical anarchist tradition of Kropotkin, Godwin and Thoreau. Their utopia is essentially one which minimizes hierarchy and authority. But others have more in common with Hobbes. Their utopia is one which stresses order and control: the pursuit of the greater good requires the control and limitation of individual liberties.

The point is this. There is a tendency for utopias as well as for ideologies to take for granted their self-evident attraction. Environmentalists like other utopians frequently present their version of heaven on earth in a way which implies that it has only to be spelled out to win over support. Of course, that is one important function of utopian thought. Individuals cannot want something until they are at least aware of its existence or possibility. There can be no will to shape history unless there are alternatives from which to choose: '. . . the complete elimination of reality-transcending elements from our world would lead us to a "matter-of-factness" which would ultimately mean the decay of the human will . . . with the relinquishment of utopias man would lose his will to shape history and therewith his ability to understand it' (Mannheim, 1966, p.236). But choice implies values and preferences. And it is here that utopian thought raises questions which are quite central to any discussion of the future. Utopias preempt the debate about values. The value which they seek to maximize, and which underlies their vision of the future, is authoritatively given and beyond dispute (Cotgrove 1976). So at the heart of utopian thought there is the empirical question as to what are the values which underlie future preferences, and how can consensus be achieved? What kind of society do people want? And what kind of society would they like if they were more aware of alternatives and possibilities? There is little doubt that one person's heaven is another's hell.

PATHS TO UTOPIA

The second problem in thinking about the future is the practicality of any particular utopia. Again, one of the shortcomings of much utopian thought is that it says very little about how we get from here to there. There are in fact a limited number of paths to utopia (Boguslaw 1965). The first of these is *blueprintism*, exemplified by the Club of Rome's computer models. Blueprints spell out a 'rational' model of the main parameters of the future state of the system — levels of production, population growth, resource utilization, and so on, which will ensure stability. The problem is to discover the laws and regularities which govern the system. Marxism is a variety of blueprintism.[3] Such plans may fail because they rest on faulty assumptions about human nature and how individuals will respond to new situations. More fundamentally, like all models, they abstract from total reality only those variables which can be handled by the model. So the Club of Rome models omit values and value change, and any exploration of political systems and processes which would play a key role in the transition to a steady state economy.

A second approach Boguslaw labels *heuristic programming*. This lays down general principles as guides to action — as bench marks against which policies can be judged. So strategies are judged according to the degree to which they contribute towards the achievement of some desirable end-state, such as justice. The great political charters and manifestos are examples: 'life, liberty, and the pursuit of happiness', or 'liberty, equality, and fraternity' provide banners beneath which supporters can be recruited and unified. The problems arise in definitions of what constitutes liberty, how it can best be safeguarded, and its relative importance in relation to other values such as equality. However, the attraction of principled programmes is that they do leave open the extremely difficult questions of strategies and practicalities to political debate and negotiation, while seeking to provide consensus on broad goals and objectives.

The third path to utopia is what Boguslaw calls the *operating unit* approach. This essentially argues that if you get the people right, the system will look after itself. It begins with people or machines carefully selected or tooled to possess certain performance characteristics' (*ibid.*, p.17). A good example is *Walden Two*, the utopia written by the behavioural psychologist, Skinner (1948). There is no problem of order in this utopia because everyone has been programmed to respond appropriately to the rewards built into the system. External constraints are minimal. Children are educated in nurseries from an early age to behave in a way which is rational and sensible for their society. Quite simply, it has been set up in such a way that no one wants to 'buck the system'. All is harmony and peace.

THE REINSTATEMENT OF POLITICS

One has only to spell out the problems of mapping the paths to utopia to become aware of the intractable difficulties. All involve major feats of social engineering. We simply do not know enough about what will work and what are the costs of any system of peace and harmony in terms of sacrifices to human potential. There has been no lack of human experimentation. Indeed, industrial society has spawned a massive proliferation of utopian experiments, though these have attracted relatively little attention from the social sciences.[4] Yet it is remarkable that any systematic analysis of these and the lessons to be learned are almost totally ignored by modern utopians. Few in the environmentalist movement, for example, have tried to discover any lessons to be learned from the more long-lived communitarian experiments of the nineteenth century, or the recent kibbutzim in Israel, or the communities which sprang up in the late 1960s. Yet these were all experiments in small-scale self-sufficiency. Nor has there been much attention to anthropological evidence although the pages of *The Ecologist* do include attempts to draw lessons for social stability from tribal societies.

But by far the most serious difficulty with utopian thought is that in the pursuit of harmony and order there is no place for conflict and dissent.

Harmony is achieved through value and normative consensus (Dahrendorf 1968).[5] By social conditioning, selection, and social engineering, all agree on the dominant goals and the rules by which they are to be achieved. And here is the clue. They are essentially de-politicized societies. Politics is the forum for the negotiation and allocation of values. And if society is not to ossify into rigid forms, if it is to adapt to a changing environment, there must be adequate mechanisms to maintain the delicate balance between stability and change, conflict and consensus. The challenge of the environmentalist movement is to ask whether society is learning the right lessons. Political systems which are insufficiently sensitive and open run the risk of the build up of frustrations and explosive reactions. The pointers are that to judge from the reactions to environmentalist critiques, some sections of society may be responding with a degree of rigidity and repression which indicates inflexibility in the face of the possible need to change and adapt. This is a central issue to which we must return. But first it is necessary to look in more detail at specific theories of the direction of change in industrial societies.

TOWARDS A POST-INDUSTRIAL SOCIETY?

The environmentalists' vision of the future arises in part from their evaluation of the present, and in part from their social paradigm—about what is desirable, and how this can be achieved. The same can be said for alternative visions. All are rooted in some evaluation of the present, and in a social philosophy of the present—a set of beliefs about how present society works, or fails to work. Prescriptions for the future understandably derive from diagnoses of the present. Values, interests and ideologies provide guidelines for thinking about the future. But they also act as blinkers.

One of the most influential views about the direction of social change is the theory that advanced industrial societies are moving into a qualitatively different phase—a post-industrial society. Since, as we have seen, the environmentalist movement is critical of industrialism, a post-industrial future could conceivably come some way towards the kind of society they want. An analysis of the theories of post-industrialism will therefore provide a point of departure.

There is much in the writings of post-industrial theorists with which environmentalists would be sympathetic or even strongly support. Indeed, one of the major environmentalist journals, *The Ecologist*, has as its sub-title 'Journal of the Post Industrial Age'. Central to the thesis is a change in the goals of society from growth to improvement, from quantity to quality. The argument takes various forms. Bell's study *The Coming of Post-Industrial Society* is perhaps the most influential, but the writings of Galbraith, Schumacher, and Dahrendorf all share common ground with much of Bell's thesis.[6] Bell's case rests heavily on the argument that post-industrial society is the next stage of development of industrial society and reflects powerful trends, the most important of which is the gradual decline in the central role of secondary production and the steadily increasing importance, both numerically and strategically, of the tertiary or service sector. With the advance of industrialization, industrial production depends increasingly on experts of all kinds—professionals, engineers, scientists, technicians. This change is reflected in the stratification and political system: the men of knowledge constitute the emergence of a new dominant class, a new potential ruling class (Bell 1974, p.109). The transfer of power to this new class is enabled by the changing needs of society, which are increasingly for the provision of non-material services, such as the protection of the environment and the public provision of needs which cannot be met by private individuals. In other words, there is a change in the dominant goals and values of society away from production and efficiency to non-economic values (pp.42–43). 'We now move to a communal ethic . . . a turn to non-capitalist modes of social thought' (p.298).

There is much else, of course. But the important questions are not perhaps details of the precise scenario, but rather the politics of the process of change. The picture which Bell paints is of an evolutionary, rather than a revolutionary process. Firstly, the knowledge class becomes gradually more important and therefore influential. And secondly, the free-enterprise society no longer satisfies the needs of the citizenry. Dahrendorf (1975) admits uncertainty about the politics of change, and looks to progressive elements in the establishment, the media, and students all to exert pressures towards an improving society. Galbraith (1974) diagnoses the end of traditional market individualism, the dominance of economy by the corporations, and the need for the reassertion of politics over economics. But he too gives little guidance on the mechanisms of transformation. Despite these shortcomings, if the thesis could be substantiated as a plausible and probable scenario, it would go far towards indicating that society was moving in the direction desired by environmentalists.

The thesis has been criticized on a number of grounds, notably in the writings of Kumar (1978) and Gershuny (1978). The critique is in part a questioning of the empirical basis of the theory, and in part doubts about the weight of interpretation which has been placed on empirical trends and especially the extent to which the trends in industrial societies support the view that the discontinuity between the present and the future justifies its evaluation as a qualitative change to a distinctly different kind of society. On all these grounds, the case can be found wanting. Firstly, there is no doubt that in all industrial societies, the long-term tendency is for the majority of the population to be employed in the tertiary service sector rather than manufacturing. But this is not as radically new as it appears. There seems never to have been a time in the last two centuries when agriculture and the services combined did not outweigh manufacturing, both in terms of the percentage employed and contribution to the national income (Kumar 1978m p.445). Secondly, the growth in the service sector in no way implies any decline in business and the market. It represents rather the growth of new industries—

entertainment, recreation and tourism—and in the private enterprise provision of health and welfare services. The increase in *tertiary occupations* is not denied. But these have been employed in production, not in personal service occupations. On the contrary, there has been a decline in the proportion of expenditure on services from 13.1 per cent in 1954 to 12.1 per cent in 1974, for education and medicine from 1.0 per cent to 0.9 per cent (Gershuny 1978, p.77). It is such evidence which leads Gershuny to conclude that 'the future of our society lies not, as Bell suggests, in the provision of services and amenities, but rather, as now, in the provision and consumption of ever more goods' (*ibid.*, p.91). The trend which he detects is towards what he describes as a 'self-service economy', in which there is increased purchase of consumer durables to permit the domestic provision of services. His scenario is for the increasing employment of tertiary occupations in the manufacturing sector.

Any increase in the numbers of professional and technical employees does not necessarily point to any change in the ethos of society through the growing political influence of a group whose values differ significantly. Many of these, as we have seen, are employed in the market sector. It is in the personal service and public sector that non-economic criteria operate most strongly. As we have argued in Chapter 3, it is these occupations which are the carriers of a non-market ethic of service. So it is confusing to refer to census data on the growth of so-called professional and technical occupations without taking account of the proportion employed in activities relating to the production and consumption of goods. Moreover, a high proportion are teachers, social workers and ancillary health workers, who can hardly be seen as wielding power and influence and constituting Bell's new knowledge class. The majority occupy subordinate positions—as employees in the hierarchies of public and private bureaucracies. Even the more highly qualified engineers and scientists in industry and public service are (willingly or not) 'servants of power' rather than autonomous professionals (Figure 5.2).

In the light of such considerations, Kumar rejects Bell's insistence on the increasing influence of a scientific and professional ethos concerned with non-market communal planning to maximize welfare. On the contrary, 'almost every feature of Bell's post-industrial society can be seen as an extension and distillation of Weber's account of the relentless process of rationalization in Western societies' (p.46). Weber's picture of the process of industrialization is one in which technical reason replaces politics, and the sphere of culture as the realm of the free creation of values shrinks. In short, so-called post-industrial society can be seen rather as the evolutionary culmination of industrialization.

If by post-industrial society we mean one in which growth has been replaced by qualitative improvement, then this would involve a radical transformation. It is doubtful whether that is in fact the trend. Firstly, the increasing numbers in tertiary 'service' occupations are employed predominantly in the wealth producing market sector rather than in welfare. There is no evidence of any dramatic increase in the rise of an autonomous professional class committed to the advancement of non-economic values. And even if there were, the evidence could hardly support the conclusion that such a new knowledge class could wrest political power and influence from the wealth producers. This would indeed amount to nothing more nor less than a silent revolution. We will return later to what we see as a central issue for the future—a power struggle between those whose interests are in wealth production and those who value welfare in its broadcast sense. The further argument that demand is shifting from goods to services is again problematic. All the signs are that industrialism is very firmly in the saddle (Kumar 1978), and that what Bell calls a post-industrial society would be more accurately described as a late-industrial society.

THEORIES AND MODELS OF CHANGE

Underlying the bewildering variety of scenarios for the future there are implicit or explicit models and theories of social change. The dominant sociological mode sees society as essentially systemic in character. That is to say, the various elements hold together in a more or less coherent way. Theories differ according to which element in the social system is identified as the prime mover. For Marx, of course, this was the mode of production: the political, legal and cultural systems simply reflected the economic structure. The functionalist model which has been so influential in the post-war period stressed the centrality of culture and argued that consensus over values ensured the integration of the social system. What both the Marxist model of antagonistic classes and the functionalist consensus model have in common is the view that the key to the whole is to be found mainly in one of the parts, and that the social system is moving, sooner or (for Marx) later towards an equilibrium in which there a conjunction or fit between the parts. They are all essentially organic views of the social system. Indeed, the organic metaphor has probably been one of the most powerful in the history of social thought.[7]

As we have seen, the most widely accepted model locates the lever of change in the techno-economic system. This is certainly the theory implicit in the dominant social paradigm and is shared by vulgar Marxism. This view takes it more or less for granted that the other aspects of the social system will respond to the imperatives generated by the economy and technology. There is of course a normative assumption generally implicit in this model, that other parts of the social system should be encouraged and tailored to fit. The other major contender is the cultural theory which locates the major sources of stability and change in the values and beliefs of dominant groups. Again, there is a normative dimension which prescribes changes in values as necessary for social stability.

We could try to answer the question of which is the most plausible theory of change. Alternatively, we could attempt the more modest task of constructing a model of the system as the necessary preliminary step before the much more difficult task of assigning values to the parameters. And it is here that the evidence points to the possibility that the organic model may be in need of revision. Take, for example, the relationship between culture and social structure. The evidence explored in previous chapters points strongly to several conclusions. Firstly, there is a lack of consensus on values and beliefs about the working of political and economic institutions. Secondly, such differences reflect the complexity of the social structure. In whatever sense we may speak about the centrality and dominance of the economic/production functions in industrial society, there are other subsystems, such as the family and welfare, which are oriented towards different goals and legitimated by different values and beliefs. From this perspective society looks less systemic and organic: it directs attention to the existence of disjunction rather than conjunction. There are two possibilities. It may be that the disjunction or lack of fit between the various institutional areas (or realms as Bell calls them) have been a persisting feature of industrial society, but hidden from view by the influence of organic models which focused attention on the evidence for conjunction and under-estimated disjunction. The Marxist model has of course emphasized disjunction and conflict between antagonistic classes, but against a background of an essentially organic model; arguing that the ideological and institutional superstructure is largely moulded in the interests of the dominant class, so that for example, the welfare sector is described as being limited to the reproduction of labour. This fit may be forced, but it is there. The alternative is that the disjunction is emerging as a feature of late capitalism/industrialism, or at least a latent disjunction is surfacing.

A CRISIS OF CULTURE?

Bell, in his *Cultural Contradictions of Capitalism* (1976), argues that whatever may have characterized previous societies, contemporary society is marked by a disjunction between the techno-economic system rationally organized to maximize utility, the polity concerned with social justice and power, and the cultural realm which he identifies as the symbolic exploration and expression of meaning in the expressive arts and religious ritual. Each realm has its own rhythm of change and there are no determinate relations between the realms. Indeed, he argues for the substantial autonomy of culture (in the restricted sense in which he is using the concept). It is this disjunction between culture and the social system which is Bell's particular focus. Here he takes a broadly Weberian line in spelling out the contradiction between culture which is 'concerned with the enhancement and fulfilment of the self and the "whole" person' (p.14) and techno-economic system in which social relationships are reified, individuals act roles and do not function as persons. It is these conflicts which are expressed as alienation, depersonalization and the attack on authority.

This perspective comes close to a thread of social criticism which runs through the history of industrialization. It is the view that there is a conflict between the expressive and moral nature of man, the pursuit of human excellence, and the demands of industrialization. It underlines the famous conflict between Snow and Leavis in the *Two Cultures* debate. It is the view that intellectuals are carriers of values which run counter to utilitarian bourgeois values (Kristol 1979), what Lionel Trilling (1961) has called an adversary culture.

Bell's focus is on the more extreme manifestations of the 'counter-culture'. What is important here is that Bell clearly identifies this as an anti-bourgeois culture. He argues too that 'change(s) in consciousness — in values and moral reasoning — is what moves men to change their social arrangements and institutions' (p.479). Indeed he goes further and considers that the existence of opposing cultures constitutes a crisis for capitalist society which will deepen with the advance of post-industrial society. 'The lack of a rooted moral belief system is the cultural contradiction of the society, the deepest challenge to its survival' (p.480).

A similar disjunction is described by Heilbronner (1976) who identifies what he describes as a decline in the business civilization, with its emphasis on the rational and calculating pursuit of wealth. He considers it possible 'that we stand on the threshold of an era in which deep seated changes in lifeways will undermine capitalism in a manner as fatal as the most dramatic proletarian revolution' (p.46). But unlike Bell, who locates the roots of an adversary culture in a new class which dominates the media and culture, Heilbronner traces the roots of a much more general disenchantment with business civilization, an exhaustion of the spirit of capitalism, to fundamental changes facing the system. The first of these is the end of the era of growth and expansion — for a variety of reasons, including not only environmental limits to growth, but the intractable problems of maintaining levels of productivity and profitability.[8] 'Few defenders of capitalism have tried to justify the system in terms of the nobility of its motivations or the spirituality of its aims. The defense of capitalism has always rested on the social contentment that was presumed to result from the release of mankind from its historic condition of material insufficiency' (p.112). Yet despite its prodigious achievements, there are increasing doubts about the hollowness of preoccupation with material goods, the failure of the business civilization to generate the satisfactions we expect. Specifically Heilbronner refers to the substitution of impersonal values for personal ones, for instance in the commercialization of sport in which 'athletes are no longer heroes but money makers' (p.113). Secondly, there is the disregard by the business civilization of the value of work, which is regarded as a means to an end and subordinated to the calculus of technical efficiency. Thirdly, there is a loss of confidence in the market mechanism, its tendency to create extremely skewed distributions of income and property, and its failure to protect against deleterious side effects such as pollution. Finally, the driving force of entrepreneurs will have been replaced by the carefully supervised calculations of state planners at the same time that the appetite for material growth will have been forcibly repressed.

Our own analysis comes closer to Heilbronner than to Bell, in the sense that we would trace the roots of any adversary culture or cultures to more general forces at work in society rather than to the influence of a literary and artistic elite. True, the literary tradition forms part of the cultural repertoire which can be raided for legitimating symbols. We would wish to suggest that what can be described as a bourgeois culture, though it may be seen as an hegemonic culture, has always constituted only a part of a complex, and far from integrated, culture. Though the bourgeois culture or business civilization is relevant to the techno-economic system, there are other important sub-systems and groups in society such as the family which are carriers of different values (Mannheim 1953) and which legitimate different systems of action.

But more fundamentally, it can be questioned whether subordinate classes in society have ever been incorporated into the dominant ideology (Abercrombie and Turner 1978). There is certainly little sign of support from the evidence of our own survey of the general public. Moreover, the political culture of the left has always constituted an adversary culture. There is even evidence which suggests very strongly that sections of the dominant strata in Britain have never fully embraced the ethos of industrialization, certainly to the same extent as in other industrialized societies (Weiner 1981).

All the signs then point to the disjunction between culture and society as a persisting feature of industrial societies. The dominant interests in industrial society never succeeded in imposing their world view on subordinate strata. And in Britain it could well be that elements of pre-industrial values resisted the complete enculturation of the dominant industrial strata so that the process of industrialization was pursued with less single-mindedness, and its impact softened. This could explain Britain's relative economic decline, as well as the fact that the expressions of our adversary culture in the shape of an aggressive youth and environmental movement has been more muted and less strident, simply because environmental and related values have not been so ruthlessly ignored in the pursuit of material goals in Britain as elsewhere. In other words, Britain may already be on the road to a 'post-industrial' society.

However, there is little doubt that the rise of the radical environmentalist movement from the late 1960s has provided a vehicle for the resurgence of an anti-business culture, always latent and periodically surfacing. And there is little doubt too that dominant business and industrial interests have felt themselves under attack. For example, Paul Johnson, in a spirited defence of industrial capitalism to the Bank Credit Analyst Conference in the U.S.A., concluded that

'. . . the free enterprise idea is losing, if it has not already lost, the intellectual and moral battle . . . the steady diffusion of ideas hostile to our free system continues remorselessly. Industrial capitalism, the free market system, is presented as destructive of human happiness, corrupt, immoral, wasteful, inefficient, and above all, doomed. Collectivism is presented as the only way out compatible with the dignity of the humane spirit and the future of our race' (*The Times*, 19 October 1978).

COALITIONS AND CONSTITUENCIES

The basic conflict is between market and non-market values and institutions. At its most stark, it is a conflict between wealth and welfare: between those for whom the dominant goal is the production of goods and services for sale, and those who wish to see wealth production subordinated to broader social goals — what Dahrendorf calls 'the improving society'. As we have said, such a change would strike at the heart of the dominant interests and is totally opposed by the dominant legitimating paradigm. Indeed, welfare is seen as the enemy of wealth, sapping initiative and enterprise, parasitic on the wealth producers, syphoning skills and resources which should be more profitably channelled into the private productive sector. It is here, then, that there is the possibility of a class conflict, in which interests align somewhat differently than in the traditional left/right dichotomy (Figure 6.1). The constituency interested in welfare is wider than the unemployed, the sick and the elderly. It includes all those employed in the public sector as hospital porters, technicians, teachers and social workers. It is more than the professionals, academics, and media personnel. It is all those affected by public sector spending and the arguments that this must be cut to facilitate 'wealth creation' in the sense of profitable market products.

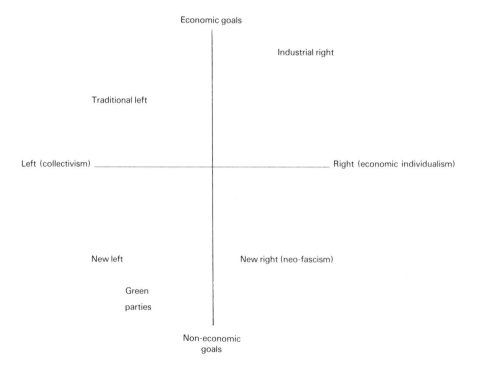

Figure 6.1. New political alignments

What is the possibility then of new alignments and coalitions? As we saw in the last chapter, there is a considerable intersection of interests between the traditional left and the so-called 'new left' as exemplified by the environmentalists. The argument for the emergence of a 'new politics' rests heavily on the researches of Inglehart and his associates which have provided evidence that a younger, more highly educated generation, has shifted its priorities from material to post-material goals. But as our analysis suggests, the left has always attached importance to non-material goals. The emergence of post-material vaues into politics may not therefore be as novel as some claim. But whether the ideology of the left has the potential to act as a bridging culture, mediating between the opposing business culture and the ideologies of the new left, is problematic.

In the past left wing analysts have been critical and even hostile towards environmentalist policies. They have accused them of being concerned with protecting the playgrounds of the middle class to the neglect of the severe environmental degradation of working class urban conditions, and with ameliorative policies rather than with identifying the structural sources of environmental damage (Enzensberger 1974). And there is a continuing tendency for Marxist writers to attribute environmental problems to the capitalist mode of production. But the possibilities of alliances between the new radical environmentalism and the left are considerable (Gale 1980). Firstly, the new environmentalism is much more concerned with a range of issues such as waste, energy conservation, and urban transport with which the left can find common cause. Secondly, the new environmentalism is rooted in a radical critique of many facets of industrial capitalism. Although their beliefs point to the need for social transformation, environmentalists have generally failed to go on to make the necessary analysis of the structural changes which would be necessary. But in their concern to increase involvement and participation, and to achieve a meaningful dialogue on, for example, nuclear power, and in their anxiety about the centralizing and alienating tendencies of high technology, there is the basis for convergence.

The main stumbling block to coalitions with the left is the extent to which the environmentalist movement has made limits to growth a central issue in recent years. Growing unemployment plus the energy crisis have contributed to a decline in the influence of the movement, especially in the U.S.A., where organized labour sees itself to be threatened with bearing the indirect costs of environmental reform (Buttel 1980).[9] There are signs, however, of a shift of emphasis towards conservation and the adoption of 'soft' technologies — those which are less resource consuming and environmentally damaging (Mitchell 1980). Such a shift could win more support among organized labour with its ambivalent attitude towards technologies which threaten the skills, health or safety of workers. Where coalitions are especially possible is around the kinds of institutional changes on which both groups might achieve some measure of agreement — specifically the modification of hierarchical authority structures by the development of processes permitting greater degrees of participation and involvement; and the moderation of market forces where these threaten the public interest, plus greater attention to non-economic 'welfare' goals in the broadest sense. But any such political alignments face the probability of alienating allies among the traditional conservationists.

The implications of environmentalism for political affiliations and alignments are clearly extremely complex. The traditional left will see nothing particularly new in the present situation. There have always been radical middle class intellectuals who have provided the left with ideological analysis. Others will see in the post-1960 events the emergence of a new left and a new politics, feeding new demands into the political system, cutting across the traditional class alignments of left and right (Barnes and Kaase 1979; Marsh 1980). All that this study can do is to underline the evidence for the growth of 'middle class radicalism', embodying a distinctive ideology which is antagonistic to industrial capitalism. Whether it can form alliances with the traditional left, or with some newly emerging alliance of the centre, is a question for the future. But it would be a matter of concern if a politically articulate, literate, and potentially influential group were to find itself isolated and not understood.

The difficulties should not be minimized. The so-called 'green' parties, which have emerged mainly in continental Europe in recent years, have been described by Dahrendorf as combining romantic conservatives and disillusioned socialists:

'The Greens are essentially about values: an imprecise, emotional protest against the allegedly overbearing rationality of the social democratic world' (Dahrendorf 1980 p.12).

Electoral alliances have generally proved to be unstable. But 'green' parties attract electoral support from only a small proportion of environmentalists. What is being explored here is the possibility of more broad based alliances which would attract the support of 'middle class radicals'.

THE POLITICS OF SCARCITY

Whether the Catastrophists are right or not, it is certainly plausible to argue that industrial societies are entering a new phase in which they will face increasing shortages of energy and raw materials and in which the long period of sustained economic growth is at an end. The way in which they adapt could well be shaped significantly by their dominant political groupings and specific patterns of coalitions.

Scarcity and the absence of growth are likely to exacerbate problems of distribution and social justice. It has been widely argued that only social democratic governments of the left will be able to ensure an appropriate economic and technological response while at the same time pursuing egalitarian policies in the distribution of increasingly scarce resources (Stretton 1976; Schnaiberg 1980). The policies of the right, it is claimed, will impose unequal sacrifice, and will lead to increasingly Draconian and authoritarian regimes.

Buttel and Larson (1980) have developed a somewhat more sophisticated model which attempts to identify in greater detail the different possible coalitions of interests within governments of left, right and centre. Firstly, it is necessary to distinguish between the monopoly and the competitive sectors of the economy. State policies tend to be biased towards monopoly sector firms, since they offer the greatest possibility for growth. Secondly, there is the distinction between the administrative state structure, made up of the bureaucratic agencies through which political decisions are channelled, and the democratic structures of representative government, through which some measure of popular control is expressed. Scarcity would generate conflicts of interest between capital and labour on the allocation of resources between production and consumption. In this conflict, the coalitions formed by monopoly sector capital and monopoly sector labour will be pivotal.

In political systems of the right (such as Japan) Buttel and Larson argue that the most likely coalitions are between monopoly sector capitan and the middle class and with the administrative sector of the state, leading to a fusion of corporate and state decision-making structures. The probable solution to scarcity, they argue, would be for the state to assume centralized relatively authoritarian control, with resource decisions made by a knowledgeable managerial elite of 'ecological mandarins'. A decrease in the standard of living would be central to a policy of frugality in order to channel resources from consumption and welfare to production, with inegalitarian consequences (Stretton 1976).

In the leftist political system (exemplified by Sweden), the most important coalition is between monopoly sector and competitive sector labour and the middle class, in order to mobilize electoral support for social democratic or radical parties. The two major fractions of capital are likely to enter into a coalition to present a common cause to the administration. The response of left systems to scarcity would tend to emphasize egalitarian solutions, and to promote a broader participation in decisions on allocation and use of natural resources.

In what Buttel and Larson call centrist type systems, the predominant coalition is between monopoly sector labour and monopoly sector capital, which in its most advanced form becomes a corporatist state, with the incorporation of labour leaders into the administration. The working class is therefore divided, and the more cohesive administrative sector is relatively powerful in relation to the democratic sector. Policies in the face of scarcity would concentrate on the reduction of waste and wise management, with the state being responsible for balancing competing demands.

Where our analysis differs from Buttel and Larson is in the role of the middle class. Their scenarios are built on the notion of the structural ambiguity of the middle class; whereas we have identified environmentalists as drawn from a distinct fraction of the middle class, not directly or indirectly involved in the production of wealth, and whose interests therefore diverge from those so involved. We have also drawn attention to the division within the working class between those with an interest in production and those whose economic interests are the provision of various non-market 'welfare' services. This suggests that the 'new' middle class by this definition would be likely to seek alliances with whatever sectors of labour see themselves as threatened by dominant economic interests. So, for example, the increasing impact of new technologies on employment could result in environmentalists and trade unionists both seeking to subordinate technology in the interest of broader objectives. And under conditions of economic decline, the new middle class could converge with those of non-market labour in resisting cuts in welfare.

THE POLITICS OF NUCLEAR POWER

The more immediate issue providing a focus for environmental concern and action is nuclear power. This has the potential for politicizing and mobilizing a wider constituency cutting across the traditional left/right division in politics (Chapter 1). Nuclear power, because of the complexity of the technology and its potential impact, spans a wide range of issues and conflicts of interests and values. It raises technical issues of safety and the risk of catastrophe, dangers from radiation and the disposal of waste. It raises economic issues about the relation between energy and growth, and about the value of economic versus other goals. It raises political questions of participation and involvement versus centralized highly technical decision-making; and it raises the fear of the plutonium economy, in which the risks of the misappropriation of fissile material, terrorism and proliferation, generate profound anxieties about intolerable incursions into privacy and liberty. But precisely because it cuts across traditional left/right divisions, there is no strong and developed basis for protest within existing party systems (Nelkin and Pollak 1980b).

The political significance and impact of protest has been, and will continue to be, shaped by particular historical and political contexts. The first phase of protest in Britain, from 1970 to 1975, concentrated on legal action, lobbying and representation, culminating in the Windscale inquiry. But, as we saw in Chapter 5, the exasperation of the protesters at the way their evidence was handled accelerated the radicalization of opposition and strengthened the resort to direct action (Marsh 1980). By contrast, opposition in France has been marked by violence and sabotage. This partly reflects the urgency with which France embarked on a massive programme of building the controversial PWR plants, in many cases close to centres of population. But there are also important aspects of governing style (Marsh 1980). By contrast with the British attempt at consensual government based on consultation, French authorities have fulfilled mandatory consultative procedures only to the lowest legal minimum, so that the French anti-nuclear movement has been effectively excluded from the decision-making process. Hence the French slogan 'electro-fascism'.[10]

What we wish to challenge above all are the charges and counter-charges of irrationality. The central argument of this analysis is to draw attention to the significance of alternative paradigms which provide frameworks of meaning. The meaning and significance of evidence can only be understood from this cultural perspective. Above all, it is differences in values (in the importance attached to political liberty compared with economic growth for example). Strong emotions are generated then in two ways. Firstly, there are the sheer frustrations generated when two world views face each other, each simply failing to understand the other. Secondly, it is not unreasonable to feel strongly when cherished values are threatened. Again, as we have argued, conflicting values present special problems, which have been almost totally ignored by political analysts. Political pluralism requires and demands coming to terms with a civic culture which is far from unified, and no longer provides a taken-for-granted consensual framework of meaning for debate.

THE POLITICS OF SOCIAL CHANGE

It is our contention that the environmentalist movement is a pointer to more broad-based social changes. Whatever convergence of events ushered in the last major change in history—the industrial revolution—there is little doubt that an essential ingredient was the 'spirit of capitalism'. And all the signs are that it is this spirit of capitalism which is losing its grip on the minds and imaginations of many. Not that it ever captured everybody. But the indications are that there is a change of mood: a weakened commitment to materialism, and to a narrowly technical rationality, and a loss of confidence in political institutions (Heilbronner 1976; Dahrendorf 1980). Political systems will therefore be greatly weakened in their ability to face problems of scarcity, unemployment and economic decline. We are less sanguine than many that political systems of the left will be more successful in avoiding authoritarian sollutions. And there are other possible reactions to economic crisis and a loss of political confidence. There could be a retreat to nationalism, or the search for new faiths, religious or secular, to replace the existing out-moded culture (Heilbronner 1976, p.117).

The fundamental problem is not so much to try to predict the direction of social change, though we may be able to get some sort of feel for the direction in which change is pointing. The problem is rather to ask whether political institutions will be able to stand the undoubted strains (Lindberg 1976). The industrial revolution was also a political revolution. A 'post-industrial' revolution could have similar consequences. The writing is on the wall that change is needed. In all industrial societies there is an increase in direct political action. We cannot agree with the conclusion of Barnes and Kaase (1979) who '. . . find no evidence of an imminent breakdown of those Western democracies because of a declining legitimacy' (p.523). The increase in direct action, they argue, represents an expansion in the repertoire of essentially democratic processes of participation and influence. The challenge is to political institutions to incorporate and thus legitimate the new forms of political influence. Moreover, they stress that the values of the 'new politics' are strongly related to pro-democratic attitudes. So while we would agree that post-materialism could point to more benign forms of politics, much will depend on the way in which dominant interests are able to incorporate what could well be seen as a fundamental and *illegitimate* threat to their interests and its ideological justification. There would be nothing particularly benign, for example, about steady but inexorable pressures on universities to control and contain 'subversive' departments and to stress studies which support the business culture. Moreover, we are less sanguine than Barnes and Kaase that broadening the basis of democratic decision-making by incorporating a wider repertoire of protest behaviour will be sufficient to ensure the legitimacy of decisions.

The problems facing the political system are much more than simply its failure to provide adequate machinery for the articulation of interests. Direct action tackles only this problem — feeding issues and points of view into the system, and making sure that the demands of interest groups adopting what Wedgwood-Benn has called 'stiletto heel' tactics, make their point of view heard. The politics of direct action contributes nothing to the major function of the political system — the aggregation of competing and conflicting demands into coherent policies which involve the ordering of priorities in the pursuit of higher order political values. The politics of confrontation, direct action and outsider politics offer no solution to this. Such tactics may succeed for single issue campaigns, such as votes for women. But the fundamental political issues raised by the 'new politics', with its shift away from an over-riding preoccupation with 'wealth creation', can only be resolved within the political system itself.

Present structures are ill-adapted to the much more fundamental task of aggregating conflicting and competing demands into broad based policies which, though they cannot satisfy all, are at least seen to be reasonable and legitimate. It is difficult to see how a predominantly two-party system can continue to cope with the new political problem of changing values. As the debate on the Cow Green reservoir illustrates so well, it is the dominant faith which always wins. Its critics are in the same position as permanent religious minorities. Unless there is the possibility for evolutionary change, there is always the danger of disruption and revolutionary change. If a conflict of values is to be resolved in the only way in which peaceful and legitimate change is possible, it can only be within the political system. Environmentalists and ecologists may well be a minority. But it is better that their voice is heard within legislatures. Political parties are the essence of the democratic process. If minority parties are prevented from forming effectively and having a voice where it counts, in parliaments and legislatures, then parliamentary systems will lose credibility and legitimacy.

Environmentalists and nuclear protesters face particular difficulties in getting their concerns taken up by major political parties. The virtual exclusion of nuclear power, for example, from party politics, leaves little alternative to the protesters but various forms of direct action.

Changes in the democratic representation structures and processes of government will not alone suffice. As we have seen, in Britain in particular, the administrative process operates in a way which ensures that many issues are de-politicized and fail to reach the political agenda. In an attempt to maximize consensus politics, departments seek wide consultation with the interests concerned. However satisfactory this may be on some issues, where there are fundamental conflicts of values at stake, these can well be suppressed by departmental procedures, and what are properly political issues fail to break through administrative constraints. Such fears are reinforced when we recall the very strong support for the dominant social paradigm among our sample of public officials.

There remains the 'anthropological problem', generated by conflicting political paradigms. We know of no simple answer. The issue is fundamental to any idea of a genuinely pluralist society. A system in which rival dogmas face each other incomprehensibly across the debating chamber hopefully exchanges verbal conflict for the threat of physical violence. But the problem is much more fundamental than the 'two cultures' debate of a decade ago. To expose arts students to some numeracy and science students to literacy simply rests on an inadequate diagnosis of the nature and significance of cultural incomprehension. The prognosis is pessimistic. Modern society is as fraught with conflicts of secular dogma as was medieval society with religious dogma. To acquire a new world view, a change of paradigm, is comparable to a religious experience.

Perhaps this is the challenge for the educational institutions in society-in their broadest sense, which includes the media. At their best literature, the arts, documentaries, can build a cultural bridge. The listener or reader can genuinely empathize and see the world through another's eyes. Our present universities fall far short in this task. Engineers and social scientists, for example, continue to pass through separate channels, with mutual incomprehension built into their courses, erupting in occasional overt expressions of hostility and antagonism. But until the problem is recognized and there is a genuine will to solve it, there can be no progress.

CATASTROPHE OR CORNUCOPIA?

In a study of this kind we cannot contribute to reducing the uncertainties over reserves of oil, silver, copper, or the impact of CO_2 on the atmosphere, or heat pollution from increasing energy supplies from non-renewable resources. But what we can do is to emphasize that 'facts' are always interpreted within the context of frameworks of meaning. And it is here that there are the gravest causes for concern. The Cornucopians *may* be wrong in their interpretation and judgement. The fact that theirs is the dominant paradigm which provides the framework for interpretation tells us something about the power structure of society, not about the epistemological status of their systems of meaning. And recent history is not exactly on their side. In the field of energy, for example, the confident optimism of the 1960s has to some extent evaporated. This is not simply a greater readiness to recognize that the horizons of limits may be closer. And there is less confidence in the technological fix, especially in nuclear power as a source of unlimited, cheap, and safe supplies.

One of the greatest differences between Catastrophists and Cornucopians is in their trust in science and technology. Here again we may be witnessing a change in the spirit of the age. The unbounded confidence in science and technology of the 1950s and 1960s has been shaken. But more importantly, there is a recognition of limits. Exponential growth in science is no more possible than in any other area. Science is an activity which requires resources of men, materials and energy. And as knowledge advances, the amount of each required for each new step forward increases so that there are diminishing returns and a deceleration in scientific innovation (Rescher 1978). This does not necessarily imply the same slowing down in technology, where there has been dramatic progress towards processes requiring less energy and materials, in for example, enzyme chemistry and electronics. But there is certainly evidence of over-optimism in high technology (Concorde and the AGRs are but two examples).

The crucial lesson is that views of the future are rooted in systems of meaning which are social constructs and lack any firm objective certainty. They are faiths and doctrines. For those who wish to put action on a firmer footing, the lesson can only be that both doctrines, those of Cornucopians equally with Catastrophists, need to be recognized for what they are, and treated even-handedly with the same degree of scepticism and caution. But since it is the Cornucopian faith which dominates and determines outcomes, and which is supported by powerful interests, it is this which is in the most urgent need of sceptical reappraisal.

The majority in industrial society are Cornucopians and not Catastrophists. The central values of industrial society are deeply embedded in most of us through upbringing and have become institutionalized in the social structure. The business community overwhelmingly adopts a Cornucopian perspective. The most powerful influences in industrial societies support the industrialists' perception of social reality, and the values by which it is judged. From where they stand, it looks good. But the dominant view has no superior claim to truth. Nor are the central values of industrial society beyond debate. It would seem prudent, for the long term interests of us all, to pay particular attention to the warnings of the Catastrophists. The cards are stacked against them: their view of reality must struggle against considerable odds. But they *could* be right. And if their vision of the future is closer to reality, and if we ignore it, then the results could well be disastrous for the future of civilization as we know it today.

NOTES

1. For a summary and analysis of scenarios of the future, see Jahoda and Freeman (1978).
2. For an example of an ecological utopia see Ernest Callenbach's *Ecotopia* 1978.
3. This is essentially Engels' approach. In place of an idealist solution evolved out of the human brain in the pursuit of some absolute justice, reason, or truth, scientific socialism has discovered the laws governing the system. It is this 'real' basis which will replace 'the mishmash of utopian thought' (Engels 1969).
4. There are of course some notable exceptions. See for example sociological analyses of the recent commune movement by Abrams and McCulloch (1976) and Rigby (1974).
5. Karl Popper argues forcefully that utopias are essentially authoritarian and totalitarian. See *The Open Society and Its Enemies* 1945, Vol.1, Chapter 9 'Aestheticism, Perfectionism and Utopianism'.
6. For an analysis and critique, see Gershuny (1978), Chapter 2; and Kumar (1978).
7. The sociological paradigm, certainly in recent years, has also excluded any consideration of the relations between society and environment (Catton and Dunlap 1980).
8. See also Commoner (1976) for a similar argument that the productivity of capital, unlike labour, is declining.
9. The evidence in the U.S.A. indicates that the number of jobs lost by pollution control requirements is small relative to the number created (Morrison and Dunlap 1980).
10. For a more detailed analysis see Nelkin and Pollak 1980b.

Questionnaire Design and Data Analysis

Andrew Duff, Ph.D.

This section provides detailed information on the design and analysis of the questionnaire used in this study. The more general implication of the survey are discussed at length in the main part of the book, and this section can be avoided by all except the technically minded. The appendix is in four parts: sample selection and response rates, scale construction, public environmental concern, and membership of environmental groups. The first two parts are concerned with the more technical aspects of questionnaire design, whereas the last two parts present detailed analyses of two aspects of the New Environmentalism.

SAMPLE SELECTION AND RESPONSE RATES

Five main groups were selected for study:

Public

1018 names were drawn at random from the electoral registers of three towns: Bath, Oldham, and Swindon. These towns were chosen so as to provide a range of geographical location, size, and industry, but in fact there was little difference in the responses of these different towns so they were combined into a single file for the purposes of analysis. 577 completed usable questionnaires were returned, which after discounting non-contacts (due to change of address, infirmity or death), represents a response rate of 60 per cent. Questionnaires were sent to the public sample during the summer and autumn of 1979.

The public sample was compared with national data on three major socio-demographic variables: age, income and occupational sector. This was to see to what extent our sample was representative of the national population.

On age our sample was very similar to the national distribution ($\chi^2_2 = 5.22$, n.s.; source: *CSO Monthly Digest of Statistics*, July 1979, HMSO), but on income our survey was found to significantly under-represent those on low incomes ($\chi^2_4 = 29.27$, $p < 0.001$; source: *CSO National Income and Expenditure*, 1979, HMSO). Variability in the measures used as well as the difficulty of finding comparable national statistics in these inflationary times may partly reduce the significance of the difference in income distributions.

It was difficult to find measures of occupational sector (market/non-market) which were directly comparable with our data. Our choice of two industrial towns (Oldham and Swindon) may have led to a bias in favour of market sector jobs. It has been estimated that there are about nine million employees in employment in industry, and about 13 million in the service sector, in the U.K. (estimated for 1978; source *Social Trends*, Vol.8). This should be compared with our figures of 58.3 per cent in the market and 41.7 per cent in non-market occupations. Probably the underlying difference is rather less, since the national statistics include a large number of market jobs within the service sector, and it is therefore difficult to make a direct comparison.

In conclusion, it should be remembered when generalizing from our public survey data that the nation as a whole may show marginally different distributions on our scales, although temporal variations and the difficulties of comparing different measuring instruments make it impossible at this stage to tell whether such differences are real or artefacts.

Industrialists

400 names were randomly selected from the current (1974/75) editions of *Business Who's Who* and *Who's Who of British Engineers*. 220 questionnaires were returned, which was a response rate of 63 per cent after excluding non-contacts. Questionnaires were sent to the industrialists in June 1978.

Trade Union Officials

399 names were selected at random from the *Trade Union Handbook* (1979) which lists national and branch officials for all the trade unions in Britain. 286 questionnaires were returned, and after discounting non-contacts this was a very satisfactory response rate of 76 per cent. The trade union officials were sent their questionnaires in 1980.

New Environmentalists

Two national environmentalist groups were chosen to represent the New Environment Movement: the Conservation Society (founded in 1966) and Friends of the Earth (founded 1970). 567 names were randomly selected from the national membership lists, and 441 questionnaires returned to us. After discounting 11 non-contacts this results in the highly satisfactory response rate of 79 per cent. Questionnaires were distributed to these members in June 1978.

Nature Conservationists

500 names from the national membership list of the World Wildlife Fund (U.K. branch) were randomly chosen to represent the large number of groups primarily interested in nature conservation in this country. 313 questionnaires were returned, a response rate of 64 per cent after excluding non-contacts. Nature conservationists were sent their questionnaires in 1980.

SCALE CONSTRUCTION

Twelve environmentalists in the Bath area were interviewed between November 1977 and January 1978. These interviews were of varying quality and helpfulness but it was nevertheless possible to derive a pool of short statements which seemed to describe adequately various aspects of environmentalists' beliefs. The diversity of attitudes we encountered in these interviews was in keeping with our expectations that utopian environmentalists were concerned not only about the environment but also about the type of society we live in, especially its predominant materialism, economism and faith in science and technology. Their attitudes seemed to form three main clusters:

1. environmental concern (pollution, resources and energy shortages, population growth, extinction of animals and plants, soil erosion, etc.);
2. anti-industrialism (domination of nature, unpleasant work, economic indicators of well-being, materialism, lack of community, lack of participation, short-sighted government, etc.);
3. anti-science (reliance on experts, feeling that technology is out of control).

We then set out to formulate Likert scales of environmental concern, anti-industrialism, and anti-science attitudes with a view to identifying the causes underlying each. In February 1978 questionnaires were distributed to 317 students at Bath University, in order to pilot our attitude scales. 169 completed questionnaires were returned, a response rate of 53 per cent. We considered this number to be adequate for reliability analysis. The scale items and reliability coefficients for these three scales are detailed below.

With these three scales of environmental concern, anti-industrialism and anti-science, we next went on to explore ways of measuring values. We wanted some way to measure environmentalists' conception of the *ideal* society rather than simply the extent of their disaffection for various aspects of *this* society. Previous researches led us to believe that environmentalists had a well-articulated utopia or ideal society which was underlying their structure of environmentalist, anti-industrial and anti-science attitudes (Cotgrove 1976). In April 1978 questionnaires were sent to 150 Bath University students, in order to pilot two value scales. 67 questionnaires were returned, a response rate of 45 per cent. This rather low response seems to have been due to sampling only from students in science subjects, these courses having been chosen to avoid ones which were sampled in the previous pilot study.

The questionnaires sent to each of the five target groups in the main survey differed slightly as the project developed, but a core consisting of the five scales of attitudes and values, and four socio-demographic/behavioural measures were included in all questionnaires. The format of these scales and measures is detailed below.

Environmental Concern

In March 1976 a pilot questionnaire was sent to a sample of students at Bath University, and also to a number of students' parents. 198 completed questionnaires were returned, a response rate of 41 per cent, of which 36 were received from parents. The complete sample was included in a preliminary analysis. In one question we attempted to determine the level of environmental concern by exploring responses to the notion of an 'environmental crisis' — this enabled us to distinguish between groups with differing degrees of sympathy with environmentalism. In another question we asked which, if any, environmental dangers we were facing, selected from a list which seemed impressionistically to cover most of the dangers cited by environmentalists. The responses to these two questions is given in Table A.1, showing percentages selecting particular environmental dangers, firstly for the total sample and then for subsamples according to their degree of support for the idea of an 'environmental crisis'.

These results were interesting on two counts. Firstly, it was clear that the response was markedly different on items about the social environment as

Table A.1. Introductory survey: percentages selecting particular environmental dangers*

		Environmental crisis?			
Environmental danger $N =$	Total Sample (198)	Yes (49)	Probably (114)	No (25)	Don't Know (9)
Food shortages	77	75	84	56	67
Pollution	70	82	69	56	76
Social disintegration	44	55	44	28	22
Energy crisis	67	73	74	20	67
Raw materials shortages	71	73	78	36	67
Crime and violence	45	67	41	28	22
Other dangers	15	20	16	8	0
No dangers foreseeable	2	0	0	16	0

*March 1976, sample of students ($n = 162$) and students' parents ($n = 36$) at Bath University

compared to ones about the physical environment: overall, the dangers of 'social disintegration' and 'crime and violence' were selected much less often than the remaining physical dangers, where these were explicitly listed. This led us to be careful to make the distinction between dangers to the physical environment and social dangers, in subsequent trials. Secondly, we found that those who gave strong or qualified support to the idea of an environmental crisis tended to select more dangers than those who did not support the idea (K—sample median test, $\chi_2^2 = 33.46$, $p < 0.001$). This suggested that it would be feasible to construct a unidimensional scale index of environmental concern by combining separate scores on a series of environmental dangers.

The pilot environmental concern scale consisted of 21 statements about environmental dangers, taking care to refer only to dangers to the physical environment and not to the social environment. The mean scale score was significantly greater when compared with a hypothetical population of the same variance and sample size, and mean falling at the mid-point of the scale (t test, $p < 0.001$). However, it is likely that some bias was introduced by respondents showing more concern for the environment than non-respondents, and we were unable to conclude anything about the level of environmental concern amongst students. The reliability coefficient, Cronbach's alpha (McKennell 1977), for the 21-item scale was 0.851, indicating substantial homogeneity in responses between items. By successively dropping items with the weakest item–total correlation the scale reliability was maximized at the 18-item length, but we felt that the marginal improvement in scale reliability was more than offset by the loss of information incurred by dropping three scale items, and so an improved scale of 20 items (alpha = 0.853) was finally settled upon, dropping the item with the lowest item–total correlation. The 20-item environmental concern scale is shown in Table A.2.

We were unable to determine directly the extent to which the high scale reliability was due to acquiescent response, since none of the items were worded negatively. However, the extent of construct validity of the scale was tested by comparing scale scores against independent attitudinal and self-reported behavioural parameters. One question asked respondents to assess the seriousness of environmental dangers, assuming they were to occur. Those who thought that environmental dangers were more serious had higher scale scores on the environmental concern scale than those who thought such dangers were less serious ($r_s = 0.51$, $p < 0.01$). A small percentage of the student sample were already either members of environmentalist organizations or had read environmentalist journals, and this group also had higher scale scores than the rest (Mann–Whitney U test, $Z = -4.06$, $p < 0.001$). We therefore felt reasonably sure that the environmental concern scale was measuring the intended attitude dimension.

Using the results from the main survey, the environmental concern scale was factor analysed using principal factoring with iteration and varimax rotation (Nie *et al.* 1975). This procedure was carried out to see whether 'environmental concern' was multi-dimensional in nature. The factor analysis was carried out

Table A.2. The environmental concern scale*

A number of possible dangers to our environment have been identified.
Which dangers do you think are present or likely?

1	2	3	4	5
Agree strongly	Agree	Undecided	Disagree	Disagree strongly

1. Pollution is rising to dangerous levels
2. Population levels are growing to beyond what the world can support
3. Some animals and plants are being threatened with extinction
4. There are likely to be serious and disruptive shortages of essential raw materials if things go on as they are
5. There is growing damage to the environment through the excessive use of chemical herbicides and pesticides
6. There is a growing possibility of food shortages in the developed countries
7. A nuclear accident resulting in contamination of the environment is increasingly likely
8. Global weather patterns are being upset
9. Economically disruptive energy shortages are likely to become more frequent if we go on as we are
10. Our countryside is becoming more and more spoilt
11. The oceans are gradually 'dying' from oil pollution and dumping of waste
12. The fabric of our cities is slowly being destroyed by air pollution
13. We are fast using up our oil reserves
14. The structure of soil is being threatened by agricultural practices
15. There are too many food additives and impurities
16. There is a real danger that we will be unable to sustain our present rate of consumption of natural resources
17. There is too much destruction of natural habitats
18. The countryside is being threatened by roads
19. Rivers and waterways are seriously threatened by pollution
20. There is a growing likelihood of water shortages

*Cronbach's alpha = 0.853

on all groups (except nature conservationists) simultaneously (n = 1429). Three factors were obtained which together accounted for 52 per cent of the total variance. The factor loadings are given in Table A.3.

The first factor included high loadings on items which were about damage to the physical environment (pollution, pesticides, soil erosion, etc.). Items which had their highest loadings on this factor were selected to form a 10-item subscale measuring concern for environmental damage ('DAMAGE'). The alpha coefficient for this subscale was 0.868. The second factor included items which were about shortages of various kinds (raw materials, energy, oil). In this subset of items the focus was upon man's use of the environment rather than the environment *per se*. One item which might have been expected to load highly on this factor (water shortages) did not do so — in fact it loaded on the first factor on environmental damage. Possibly this might be explained by the cue 'water' conjuring up pollution rather than the intended meaning of drought as a possible object of environmental concern. The items which had

Table A.3. Factor analysis of environmental concern scale*

Item	Factor 1 (Damage)	Factor 2 (Shortage)	Factor 3 (Nature)
1	*0.55538*	0.29540	0.28867
2	0.18536	*0.42471*	0.15688
3	0.20481	0.29174	*0.43441*
4	0.19890	*0.68347*	0.22232
5	*0.50906*	0.22463	0.32245
6	0.33022	*0.47791*	0.06550
7	*0.46501*	0.21826	0.21175
8	*0.60010*	0.11006	0.03813
9	0.22153	*0.59143*	0.07452
10	0.39717	0.22284	*0.60431*
11	*0.61167*	0.23098	0.29996
12	*0.58043*	0.16946	0.24308
13	0.07772	*0.63986*	0.18091
14	*0.52277*	0.29178	0.28923
15	*0.56247*	0.16902	0.28910
16	0.19470	*0.64898*	0.27293
17	0.32730	0.26276	*0.69672*
18	0.43724	0.20837	*0.48118*
19	*0.56487*	0.16800	0.35329
20	*0.46902*	0.26976	0.14854

*For items, see Table A.2. Items used to form factor subscales are indicated by italics.

their highest loadings on this factor were selected to form a 6-item subscale measuring concern for environmental shortages ('SHORTAGE'), with an alpha coefficient of 0.787. The third factor seemed to measure concern about nature (extinction of animals and plants, spoilt countryside, destruction of habitats). These formed a short four-item scale ('NATURE') with an alpha coefficient of 0.782.

Anti-industrialism

An anti-industrialism scale consisting of 24 items was also piloted. The reliability of the scale was quite high (alpha = 0.773), but successive deletion of the weakest items resulted in a substantial improvement in reliability and a shortened scale of 20 items (alpha = 0.795) was produced since further deletions produced only very small improvements in reliability. The construct validity of this scale was tested by comparing scale scores against an independent self-rating of political preference. Those who marked themselves as left in politics tended to have higher scores on the anti-industrialism scale than those who said they were right in politics (r_s = −0.44, $p < 0.001$; individuals answering 'no position on this spectrum' were excluded).

A shortened anti-industrialism scale ('ANTIINDS') was later used in most versions of the main test questionnaire, since it was felt desirable to keep the length of the questionnaire to a minimum. Nine items were selected for this shortened scale, with an alpha coefficient of 0.615. The anti-industrialism scale items (shortened version) are given in Table A.4.

Table A.4. The anti-industrialism scale (short version)*

Here are a number of statements about the kind of society we live in. What are you opinions?

1	2	3	4	5
Agree strongly	Agree	Undecided	Disagree	Disagree strongly

1. Industrial societies are 'good' societies in that they provide a high level of well-being for most people who live in them
2. There are forces at work in modern societies which stimulate a lot of artificial wants for things that we do not really need
3. Vigorous industrial output is the mark of a health society
4. We attach too much importance to economic measures of the level of well-being in our society
5. The business community works for the good of the nation
6. The market is the best way to supply people with things they want
7. Our present way of life is much too wasteful of resources
8. On balance the advantages of cities outweigh their disadvantages
9. Too many issues are now decided by experts without sufficient consultation with those affected

*Cronbach's alpha = 0.615

Table A.5. The anti-science scale (short version)*

Here are a number of statements about science and technology. What are your opinions?

1	2	3	4	5
Agree strongly	Agree	Undecided	Disagree	Disagree strongly

1. Science and technology provide man with his best hope for the future
2. The bad effects of technology outweigh its advantages
3. Science and technology can solve our problems by finding new sources of energy and materials, and ways of increasing food production
4. We are in danger of letting technology run away with us

*Cronbach's alpha = 0.823

Anti-science

An anti-science scale of 11 items was also included in the pilot survey. This scale had a high reliability (alpha = 0.802) but an improved scale of nine items was produced by successive item deletion (alpha = 0.844). The construct validity was tested by comparing scores of students in the social sciences with those doing chemistry and engineering. Students in science courses had lower scores on the anti-science scale than those in the social sciences (Mann-Whitney U test, $Z = -4.60$, $p < 0.001$). A shortened four-item scale

('ANTISCIS') was used in most versions with an alpha coefficient of 0.823. The shortened scale items are given in Table A.5.

Post-material values

Our scale of post-material values was based on Inglehart's published account (in Lindberg 1976) in which this scale is described and theoretically justified. However, we felt that since Inglehart did not allow respondents to give equal priority to both material and post-material goals (instead requiring people to rank different goals) the degree of polarization between 'materialists' and 'post-materialists' is artificially enlarged. We used a different method of scoring which allowed people to give equal weight to material and post-material goals.

Ten Inglehart items were used in a pilot, and found to have only moderate reliability (alpha = 0.544), but two items had very low item-total correlations (< 0.1) and so an improved eight-item scale ('POSTMATM') was produced with a higher reliability (alpha = 0.584). The eight-item post-material values scale is given in Table A.6.

Table A.6. The post-material values scale*

Here is a list of possible aims for the country as a whole. What do you think this country's priorities should be for the next ten years or so?

1 High priority	2 Moderate priority	3 Intermediate/ undecided	4 Low priority	5 Very low priority

1. Maintaining a high rate of economic growth (M)
2. Giving people more say in important goverment decisions (PM)
3. Making sure that this country has strong defence forces (M)
4. Progressing toward a less impersonal, more humane society (PM)
5. Seeing that people have more say in how things get decided at work (PM)
6. Progressing towards a society where ideas are more important than money (PM)
7. Maintaining a stable economy (M)
8. Fighting rising prices (M)

*Cronbach's alpha = 0.584

Anti-Economic Values

We also constructed a scale of values by presenting a list of dichotomies which could be used to characterize a possible ideal society. The method of scoring was similar to Osgood's semantic differential technique (Osgood *et al.* 1959). The initial pool of 21 items had a high reliability (alpha = 0.778), but we finally used a shorter scale consisting of 14 items, with slightly improved reliability (alpha = 0.779). We called this a scale of opposition to economic individualism, or anti-economic values for short ('ANTIECON'). The scale items are given in Table A.7.

Table A.7. The antiecon values scale*

There may be a lot of things wrong with our present society — but what sort of things would you like to see in their place? How would you describe the *ideal* type of society, from your point of view?

For example, if you think the ideal society is one in which there is more emphasis on competition, then place a × towards the left-hand end of the scale, thus:

	1	2	3	4	5	6	7

A society in which there is more emphasis on competition, or one in which there is more emphasis on cooperation?

× competition   cooperation

1. A society in which there is a continually growing economy, or one in which there is no growth?
2. A society in which production is selective (e.g. towards products which use little energy), or one which aims to satisfy the market for consumer goods?
3. An economy geared to overcoming limits to growth (e.g. from exhaustion of some raw materials), or one which accepts that there are limits to growth?
4. A society in which the individual lives his life within a community, or one in which the individual is free to go his own way?
5. A society with strong law and order, or one which attaches relatively less importance to law and order?
6. A society in which the individual has a considerable say in how things get decided at his work-place, or one in which decisions (after consultation) are left to management?
7. A society which emphasizes work which is humanly satisfying, or one where work is controlled mainly by the needs of industry?
8. A society which emphasizes rewards for talent and achievement, or one where the emphasis is on other criteria (such as need)?
9. A predominantly capitalist society, in which market forces and private interests predominate, or a predominately socialist society, in which public interests and a controlled market predominate?
10. A society which emphasizes the social and collective provision of welfare, or one where the individual is encouraged to look after himself?
11. A society which has a strong emphasis on community and belonging, or one where the emphasis is on individualism?
12. A society which emphasizes the participation of individuals in major government decisions, or one which leaves the final decisions to the judgement of the elected government?
13. A society which strengthens the influence of experts in complex government decisions (such as nuclear energy), or one which facilitates the participation of the 'man in the street'?
14. A society which recognizes differentials related to skill, education and achievement, or one which emphasizes similar incomes and rewards for everybody?

*Cronbach's alpha = 0.779

Socio-Demographic/Behavioural Variables

The following four measures were used in all cases. Age was measured on a four-point scale with the following categories: under 21, 21–30, 31–40, and over 40. The respondent was asked to report his or her occupation in as much detail as possible and this was then coded according to whether the occupation was in the market sector (= 1) or in the non-market sector (= 2) and whether it involved a position of dominance, subordination, or autonomy. Political preference was elicited using a six-point self-rated left–right scale with the categories being left, mildly left, centre, mildly right, right, and 'no position on this spectrum'. Responses were recoded so that a high score corresponded to increasing political liberalism, and those responding 'no position' were regarded as having a missing value on the politics scale. Respondents were asked whether they would support direct action over environmental issues, with the following question:

'What is your attitude towards taking direct action in order to influence government decisions on issues such as siting airports, nuclear power stations, roads? Would you support such action, or do you think people should restrict themselves to working through the normal political channels, such as parties and pressure groups?'

Responses ranging from 'strongly support' (1) to 'strongly opposed' (5) were allowed.

Various other measures were given to particular groups. These were: sex, number of years further education, number of O-levels, number of A-levels, number of CSEs, certificate or diploma, first degree, higher degree, type of industry, income per annum, whether active in politics, whether would vote in an election, political party preference, whether environmental policy influences choice of party, whether environmental policy influences voting behaviour, whether a member of any environmentalist organization, membership of: Conservation Society, Ecology Party, Friends of the Earth, other society; whether reads: *Ecologist*, *Resurgence*, *Undercurrents*, *Vole*, other journal.

PUBLIC ENVIRONMENTAL CONCERN

There has been much research in the last decade into the social bases of public environmental concern, particularly in the U.S.A. (Van Liere and Dunlap 1980). Two main conclusions have emerged from this research. Firstly, that it is important to distinguish between different components of environmental concern, and secondly, that cognitive variables are probably just as important as socio-demographic variables in predicting public environmental concern. Here we present a multiple regression analysis of the public's scores on our three environmental concern subscales (DAMAGE, SHORTAGE, and NATURE) using age, politics, income, market–non-market occupational classification, and the four remaining attitudinal and values scales as independent variables. This enables an assessment of the relative independent contribution of each predictor variable to variation in environmental concern, as well as a measure of the proportion of total variance explained by this set of predictor variables. Finally, we discuss this analysis in the light of the American findings.

Table A.8. Zero order correlation matrix, public sample*

	X_1	X_2	X_3	X_4	X_5	X_6	X_7	X_8	X_{9a}	X_{9b}	X_{9c}
X_1 = Age	..										
X_2 = Politics	-154	..									
X_3 = Income	071	045	..								
X_4 = Market	-007	-067	-184	..							
X_5 = Anti-ind.	-179	310	083	124	..						
X_6 = Anti-sci.	024	124	-021	197	407	..					
X_7 = Post-mat.	-175	451	-022	072	448	339	..				
X_8 = Anti-ECON	-184	561	-006	062	392	274	660	..			
X_{9a} = DAMAGE	109	-025	-219	045	217	231	230	227	..		
X_{9b} = SHORTAGE	057	089	-076	083	147	177	129	171	619	..	
X_{9c} = NATURE	083	028	-171	100	272	212	302	255	642	525	..

*Decimals omitted

The zero-order correlation matrix for all the variables included in this analysis is given in Table A.8. As expected, the three environmental concern subscales intercorrelate highly. It is noteworthy that, with one exception, cognitive variables correlate more highly with the environmental concern subscales than do the socio-demographic variables. This suggests that support for public environmental concern is more a question of support for certain values and attitudes than it is the product of a particular social group. It is also interesting to note that politics is not a consistent predictor of the three environmental concern measures.

Table A.9 gives standardized path coefficients for each of the three environmental concern subscales regressed against the eight predictor variables. The value for R^2 gives the proportion of total variance explained. This shows that there are different social sources for the three types of environmental concern.

Politics and income both have substantial effects on awareness of environmental damage, and age has a somewhat lesser effect. High scores on this scale tend to come from those who are right-wing, low-income and older than average. There is also a substantial effect of anti-economic values and holding anti-industrial beliefs. The constituency for concern about damage are the conservationists who blame industrial society and economic values for deterioration in environmental quality; these are very often elderly and retired people who hold conservative political views.

Support for the environmental shortages scale is, by contrast, not linked to politics and only very weakly to income. Similarly, age has a very weak direct effect. This sugests that people in very different social groups are concerned about shortages, perhaps for different reasons. However, anti-economic values and, to some extent, anti-science beliefs, are moderately good predictors. The low proportion of variance explained on this scale reinforces the suggestion that environmental shortages receive widespread support and are only weakly associated with any particular group.

Concern about nature is very similar to awareness of environmental damage, except that anti-industrialism and post-material values have larger

134

Table A.9. Multiple regression analysis of environmental concern subscales, public sample

Independent variable	Dependent variable		
	DAMAGE	SHORTAGE	NATURE
Age	0.179	0.097	0.170
Politics	-0.234	0.004	-0.193
Market	-0.077	0.032	-0.002
Income	-0.245	-0.081	-0.187
Antiinds	0.175	0.079	0.211
Antiscis	0.096	0.103	0.028
Postmatm	0.104	-0.021	0.197
Antiecon	0.230	0.139	0.173
R^2	0.212	0.065	0.208

direct effects relative to the effects of politics, income and age. Again, the constituency for this element of environmental concern seems to be the conservationist groups.

This analysis shows that cognitive variables have substantial direct effects on environmental concern, in addition to socio-demographic variables. These variables are also the most consistent predictors of environmental concern generally, since there are wide differences in the pattern of association between the three types of environmental concern and socio-demographic measures. Awareness of damage and concern for nature are very similar, but the constituency for awareness of shortages is very different. This implies the need to analyse different types of environmental concern separately, and not to conflate them.

Not only are there differences depending on the dimension of the environment identified (e.g. whether shortages or damage), but also depending on the way in which concern is expressed. Awareness of environmental problems needs to be distinguished from support for environmental reform (Buttel and Flinn 1976). Preliminary analysis of international survey data indicates that age and income have more effect on environmental reform than on awareness of dangers. The effect of rejection of the dominant social paradigm is even more marked for reform.

The pattern of association between environmental concern and the socio-demographics is somewhat surprising in view of American research findings. Buttel (1979) reported a significant negative direct effect of age on two indices of environmental concern, whereas we consistently found a positive effect. Similarly, it is generally reported that political liberalism is positively associated with environmental concern in America (Buttel and Flinn 1978), whereas we found the reverse effect on two of our scales, and no effect of politics on the third.

The general conclusion to emerge from this analysis is that there is no single constituency for environmental concern, whether considering this country alone or more generally to include other countries such as the U.S.A. There is little evidence to suggest that environmental concern is the exclusive preserve of a particular social group. But what this analysis does tend to suggest is that aperson's values (anti-economic, post-material) and attitudes (anti-industrial, perhaps anti-science) are the key to understanding environmental concern, and are the only attribute that these disparate groups — all environmentally concerned — hold in common.

MEMBERSHIP OF ENVIRONMENTAL GROUPS

Why do some people join environmental groups? This question can perhaps be answered by looking at the social composition, attitudes, and values of group members, and comparing them with a control sample of the general public. First of all, we shall examine the attitudinal distributions of our sample of new environmentalists: the members of the Conservation Society and Friends of the Earth.

Table A.10. Environmental concern, environmentalists and public

		Environ-mentalists %	Public %	P
Damage	Low	3	11	
	Medium	47	53	<0.001
	High	50	36	
Shortage	Low	3	21	
	Medium	40	50	<0.001
	High	57	30	
Nature	Low	0	4	
	Medium	9	30	<0.001
	High	91	66	

Table A.10 shows that environmentalists are much more concerned about the environment than the average member of the public, and that this is true of each of the three types of environmental concern we measured. It therefore seems likely that a heightened awareness of environmental problems is one of the factors that leads people to joining an environmental group. However, there are some indications that although this may be a necessary condition, it is not a sufficient condition for becoming a member. Table A.11 shows that our sample of environmentalists were also much more anti-industrial, anti-science, post-material and anti-economic than would be expected if they were randomly drawn from the general public.

Now it is probably true to say that, out of the large number of people who share environmentalists' beliefs and values, only a very small proportion will go on to join an environmentalist group. Support for voluntary organizations tends to come frm those with a higher-than-average disposable income, for example, since there is the need to find the cost of a subscription each year. So

Table A.11. Attitudes and values, environmentalists and public

		Environ-mentalists %	Public %	P
ANTIINDS	Low	2	13	
	Medium	58	81	<0.001
	High	40	6	
ANTISCIS	Low	22	68	
	Medium	61	29	<0.001
	High	17	3	
POSTMATM	Low	4	26	
	Medium	75	72	<0.001
	High	21	2	
ANTIECON	Low	11	38	
	Medium	56	57	<0.001
	High	33	5	

not only do environmental group members tend to differ from the public in terms of their environmental concern and other beliefs and values, but we can expect them to differ in their social composition as well. Table A.12 shows that environmentalists are generally younger, left-wing, employed in non-market occupations, and higher in income, than the average member of the public. Note that in the general public environmental concern tended to be associated with people who were older, right-wing and on low incomes, i.e. in the reverse direction to the social composition of the environmental groups. In fact, it seems likely that values are a better indicator of who is likely to join an environmental group, since we found (Table A.8) that support for anti-industrialism, post-material values, and anti-DSP values tended to be supported by precisely these younger, left-wing elements in society.

To summarize, support for the new environmental groups tends to come from those who are environmentally concerned and who share a set of values which are critical of industrial society with its predominant materialism and economism. Environmental concern is relatively widespread in society, but the values are quite localized and so the typical environmental group member tends to come from that section of society which supports these values: left-wing youth. Although environmental concern and the values tend to be negatively correlated with income, the typical group member tends to have a higher-than-average income, presumably because group membership entails a commitment of time and resources (for subscriptions, travelling to meetings, etc.). This suggests that there might be a large latent source of support for the environmental groups in those who are in low incomes, and that the groups would do well to consider ways of encouraging such people to join. Finally, a relatively large proportion of group members are employed in the non-market

Table A.12. Socio-demographics, environmentalists and public

		Environ-mentalists %	Public %	P
Age	<21	5	8	
	21–30	28	21	
	31–40	25	19	<0.001
	>40	42	51	
Politics*	Left	18	9	
	Mildly left	37	21	
	Centre	24	34	<0.001
	Mildly right	16	22	
	Right	5	14	
Occupation	Market	36	58	<0.001
	Non-market	64	42	
Income	<2001	17	28	
	2001–4000	32	44	
	4001–6000	24	21	<0.001
	6001–8000	15	5	
	>8000	11	1	

*Excluding 'no position on this spectrum'

sector; this is doubtless because people in this sector can 'afford' to be critical of industrial society and material and economic goals—even to the extent of openly joining an organization which proclaims such views—whereas people in market-sector jobs would experience a conflict between their values and their economic interests.

The next stage of the analysis examines the social composition of members of the World Wildlife Fund, our sample of nature conservationists, to compare with the two new environmental groups. Here we find that there are important differences.

Nature conservationists are, like the environmentalists, very concerned about the environment, though they score somewhat lower on 'shortages' (Table A.13). However, they do not entirely share the environmentalists' other beliefs and values. On anti-industrial society and post-material values the nature conservationists did not differ from the public, and were actually less likely to support anti-economic values than the public, but did tend to favour anti-science (Table A.14). The demographic data show that nature conservationists are generally older, more right-wing and on higher incomes than the public generally, but do not differ in occupational sector (Table A.15). The age and politics distributions accord well with their values, since as we have seen anti-economic values are generally restricted to left-wing youth. High incomes are what would be expected of voluntary organization members, and since they do not express anti-economic values there is no need for them to

138

Table A.13. Environmental concern, nature conservationists and public

		Nature conservationists %	Public %	P
Damage	Low	6	11	
	Medium	51	53	<0.05
	High	44	36	
Shortage	Low	10	21	
	Medium	56	50	<0.001
	High	33	30	
Nature	Low	1	4	
	Medium	9	30	<0.001
	High	90	66	

Table A.14. Attitudes and values, nature conservationists and public

		Nature conservationists %	Public %	P
ANTIINDS	Low	11	13	
	Medium	79	81	n.s.
	High	10	6	
ANTISCIS	Low	43	68	
	Medium	53	29	<0.001
	High	4	3	
POSTMATM	Low	30	26	
	Medium	66	72	n.s.
	High	3	2	
ANTIECON	Low	50	38	
	Medium	45	57	<0.01
	High	5	5	

be located mainly in non-market occupations, as were the new environmentalists.

So this piece of evidence reinforces our conviction that what distinguishes members of the new environmental groups is not their heightened environmental awareness at all, but their alternative value system. Nature conservationists are equally concerned for the environment but they differ on questions of social values. It is commitment to a set of values which explains why people join a particular group and why these different types of environmental organization should recruit different types of member. Irrespective of their level of environmental concern, people who are right-wing and not opposed to the dominant social paradigm are very unlikely to join a

Table A.15. Socio-demographics, nature conservationists and public

		Nature conservationists %	Public %	P
Age	<21	0	8	
	21–30	12	21	<0.001
	31–40	18	19	
	<40	70	51	
Politics*	Left	1	9	
	Mildly left	9	21	
	Centre	26	34	<0.001
	Mildly right	37	22	
	Right	27	14	
Occupation	Market	53	58	n.s.
	Non-market	47	42	
Income	<2001	12	28	
	2001–4000	30	44	
	4001–6000	26	21	<0.001
	6001–8000	13	5	
	<8000	19	1	

*Excluding 'no position on this spectrum'

new environmental group. Conversely, people who are left-wing, critical of industrial society, and profess anti-economic values are unlikely to join a nature conservation group, despite their high level of environmental awareness.

This conclusion is further reinforced if we compare the new environmentalists with a group which shares many of their values and beliefs. Trade union officials are closer to the new environmentalists on support for post-material values and rejection of economic individualism than they are to nature conservationists (Table 2.2). But like nature conservationists, they score low on the anti-industrial society scale, and are not anti-science and technology. So it is the complex pattern of beliefs and values which explains support. And the polarization is most marked for the group which is most antagonistic to the new environmentalism — senior industrialists.

References

Abercrombie, N., and Turner, B. S. (1978). 'The dominant ideology thesis', *Brit. J. Soc.*, **29**, 149–170.

Abrams, P. (1970). 'Rites de passage: the conflict of generations in industrial society', *J. of Contemp. Hist.*, **5**, 175–190.

Abrams, P. and McCulloch, A. (1976). *Communes, Sociology and Society*, Cambridge University Press.

Ackerman, B. A. *et al.* (1974). *The Uncertain Search for Environmental Quality*, Collier Macmillan, London.

Albrecht, S. L. (1972). 'Environmental social movements and counter-movements', *J. of Vol. Action Res.*, **1**, 2–11.

Allaby, M. (1971). *The Eco-Activists: Youth Fights for a Human Environment*, Charles Knight, London.

Almond, G. A. and Verba, S. (1963). *The Civic Culture: Political Attitudes and Democracy in Five Nations*, Princeton University Press.

Andrews, R. N. L. (1980). 'Class politics or democratic reform: environmentalism and American political institutions', *Nat. Res. J.* **20**, 221–242.

Armytage, W. H. G. (1961). *Heavens Below: Utopian Experiments in England 1560–1960*, Routledge and Kegan Paul, London.

Armytage, W. H. G. (1968). *Yesterday's Tomorrows: A Historical Survey of Future Societies*, Routledge and Kegan Paul, London.

Arndt, H. W. (1978). *The Rise and Fall of Economic Growth*, Longman, Cheshire, Melbourne.

Ashby, E. (1978). *Reconciling Man with the Environment*, Oxford University Press.

Bacon, R., and Eltis, W. (1976). *Britain's Economic Problem: Too Few Producers*, Macmillan, London.

Baker, R. J. S. (1979). 'Nuclear power: the widening debate', *Pol. Quart.*, **50**, 71–85.

Banks, J. A. (1972). *The Sociology of Social Movements*, Macmillan, London.

Barnes, S. H., and Kaase, M. (1979). *Political Action: Mass Participation in Five Western Democracies*, Sage, Beverly Hills and London.

Barr, J. (ed.) (1971). *The Environmental Handbook: Action Guide for the U.K.* (new edition) Ballantine/Friends of the Earth, London.

Bass, B. M., and Eldridge, L. D. (1973). 'Accelerated managers' objectives in twelve countries', *Industrial Relations*, **12**, 158–171.

Bell, D. (1962). *The End of Ideology: On the Exhaustion of Political Ideas in the Fifties*, Free Press, New York.

Bell, D. (1974). *Coming of Post-Industrial Society: A Venture in Social Forecasting*, Heinemann, London.

Bell, D. (1976). *The Cultural Contradictions of Capitalism*, Heinemann, London.

Benewick, R. and Smith, T. (1972). *Direct Action and Democratic Politics*, George Allen and Unwin, London.

Beresford, M. (1977). 'Doomsayers and eco-nuts: a critique of the ecology movement', *Politics*, **12**, 98–106.

Berger, P. L. *et al.* (1974). *The Homeless Mind: Modernization and Consciousness*, Penguin, Harmondsworth.

Bernal, J. D. (1939). *The Social Function of Science*, Routledge and Kegan Paul, London.

Boguslaw, R. (1965). *The New Utopians: A Study of System Design and Social Change*, Prentice-Hall, Englewood Cliffs, N.J.

Bookchin, M. (1974). *Post-Scarcity Anarchism*, Wildwood House, London.

Boulding, K. E. (1971). 'The economics of the coming spaceship earth' in J. Barr (ed.), *The Environmental Handbook: Action Guide for the U.K.* (new edition) pp.77–82, Ballantine/Friends of the Earth, London.

Bowles, S. and Gintis, H. (1978). 'The invisible fist: have capitalism and democracy reached a parting of the ways?', *Amer. Econ. Rev.*, **68**, 358–363.

Braungart, R. G. (1971). 'Family status, socialization and student politics: a multivariate analysis', *Amer. J. Soc.*, **77**, 108–130.

Braverman, H. (1974). *Labour and Monopoly Capital: The Degradation of Work in the Twentieth Century*, Monthly Review Press, London.

Brookes, L. G. (1976). 'The plain man's case for nuclear energy', *Atom*, **234**, 95.

Butler, D. and Stokes, D. (1969). *Political Change in Britain: Forces Shaping Electoral Choice*, Macmillan, London.

Buttel, F. H. (1979). 'Age and environmental concern: a multivariate analysis', *Youth and Society*, **10**, 239–256.

Buttel, F. H. (1980). 'The environmental movement: historical roots and current trends', in C. R. Humphrey and F. H. Buttel (eds.), *Environment, Energy and Society*, Wadsworth, Belmont, California.

Buttel, F. H. and Flinn, W. L. (1976). 'Environmental politics: the structuring of partisan and ideological cleavages in mass environmental attitudes', *Soc. Quart.*, **17**, 477–490.

Buttel, F. H. and Flinn, W. L. (1978). 'Social class and man's environmental beliefs', *Environ. Behav.*, **10**, 433–450.

Buttel, F. H. and Larson, W. O., III, (1980). 'Whither environmentalism? The future political path of the environmental movement', *Nat. Res. J.*, **20**, 323–344.

Buttel, F. H. and Newry, H. N. (1980). *The Rural Sociology of Advanced Societies*, Croom Helm, London.

Callenbach, E. (1978). *Ecotopia*, Pluto Press.

Carr-Saunders, A. M. and Wilson, P. A. (1933). *The Professions*, Oxford University Press.

Carson, R. (1965). *Silent Spring*, Penguin, Harmondsworth.

Carter, A. (1973). *Direct Action and Liberal Democracy*, Routledge and Kegan Paul, University of Illinois, London.

Catton, W. R. Jr. and Dunlap, Riley E. (1980). 'A new ecological paradigm for post-exuberant sociology', *American Behavioural Scientist*, **13**, 15–47.

Chamberlain, V. W. (1977). 'Attitudes towards direct political action' in C. Crouch (ed.), *Participation in Politics*, pp.163–165, Croom Helm, London.

Chisholm, A. (1972). *Philosophers of the Earth: Conversations with Ecologists*, Sidgwick and Jackson, London.

Cole, H. S. D., *et al.* (1973). *Thinking About the Future: A Critique of the Limits to Growth*, Chatto and Windus for Sussex University Press, London.

Cole, H. S. D., *et al.* (1973). *Thinking About the Future: A Critique of the Limits to Growth*, Chatto and Windus for Sussex University Press, London.

Collins, H. M. (1974). 'The TEA set: tacit knowledge and scientific networks', *Sci. Stud.*, **4**, 165–186.

Collins, H. M. (1979). 'The investigation of frames of meaning in science: complementarity and compromise', *Soc. Rev.*, **27**, 703–716.

Collins, H. M. and Cox, G. (1976). 'Recovering relativity: did prophecy fail?', *Soc. Stud. Sci*, **6**, 423–444.

Commoner, B. (1972). *The Closing Circle: Confronting the Environmental Crisis*, Jonathan Cape, London.

Commoner, B. (1976). *The Poverty of Power: Energy and the Economic Crisis*, Jonathan Cape, London.

Connerton P. (ed.) (1976). *Critical Sociology*, Penguin, Harmondsworth.

Cotgrove, S. F. (1973). 'Anti-science', *New Scientist*, July, 82–84.

Cotgrove, S. F. (1974). 'Objections to science', *Nature*, **250**, 764–767.

Cotgrove, S. F. (1975). 'Technology, rationality and domination', *Social Studies of Science*, **5**, 55–78.

Cotgrove, S. F. (1976). 'Environmentalism and utopia', *Soc. Rev.*, **24**, 23–42.

Cotgrove, S. F. (1978a). 'Styles of thought: science, romanticism and modernisation', *Brit. J. Soc.*, **29** (3), 358–371.

Cotgrove, S. F. (1978b). *The Science of Society* (4th edn.) George Allen and Unwin, London.

Cotgrove, S. F. and Box, S. (1970). *Science, Industry and Society*, George Allen and Unwin, London.

Cotgrove, S. and Duff, A. (1980). 'Environmentalism, middle class radicalism and politics', *Soc. Rev.*, **28**, 333–351.

Cotgrove, S. and Duff, A. (1981). 'Environmentalism values and social change', *Brit. J. Soc.*, **32**(1), 92–110.

Crewe, I. *et al.* (1977). 'Partisan dealignment in Britain 1964–1974', *Brit. J. Pol. Sci.*, **7**, 129–190.

Crick, F. (1966). *Of Molecules and Men*, University Press, Washington.

Crompton, R., and Gubbay, J. (1977). *Economy and Class Structure*, Macmillan, London.

Crouch, C. (ed.) (1977). *Participation in Politics*, Croom Helm, London.

Dahl, R. A. (1961). *Who Governs: Democracy and Power in an American City*, Yale University Press.

Dahrendorf, R. (1959). *Class and Class Conflict in Industrial Society*, Routledge and Kegan Paul, London.

Dahrendorf, R. (1967). *Society and Democracy in Germany*, Weidenfeld and Nicolson, London.

Dahrendorf, R. (1968). *Essays in the Theory of Society*, Routledge and Kegan Paul, London.

Dahrendorf, R. (1975). *The New Liberty*, Routledge and Kegan Paul, London.

Dahrendorf, R. (1980). *After Social Democracy*, Liberal Publication Department, London.

Dalton, R. J. (1977). 'Was there a revolution?', *Comp. Pol. Stud.*, **9**, 459–473.

Davis, K. and Moore, W. E. (1945). 'Some principles of stratification', *Amer. Soc. Rev.*, **10**, 242–249.

Davoll, J. (1976). 'Controversy over nuclear power', *J. Brit. Nuc. Energy Soc.*, **15**, 200–203.

Del Sesto, S. L. (1980). 'Conflicting ideologies of nuclear power: congressional testimony on nuclear reactor safety', *Pub. Pol.*, **28**,

Derr, T. S. (1970). 'Man Against Nature', *Cross Currents*, **20**, 243–275.

Dickson, D. (1974). *Alternative Technology: and the Politics of Technical Change*, Fontana, London.

Douglas, M. (1966). *Purity and Danger: An Analysis of Concepts of Pollution and Taboo*, Routledge and Kegan Paul, London.

Douglas, M. (1970). *Natural Symbols: Explorations in Cosmology*, Cressett Press, London.

Douglas, M. (1972). 'Environments at risk' in J. Benthall (ed.), *Ecology, The Shaping Enquiry*, Longmans, London.

Downs, A. (1972). 'Up and down with ecology: the "issue-attention cycle"', *The Pub. Int.*, **28**, 38–50.

Dubin, R. (1962). 'Industral workers worlds', in A. M. Rose (ed.), *Human Behaviour and Social Processes*, Routledge and Kegan Paul, London.

Dunlap, R. E. (1976). 'Understanding opposition to the environmental movement: the importance of dominant American values'. Paper to Annual Meeting of the Society for the Study of Social Problems New York, August.

Dunlap, R. E. and Catton, W. R. Jr. (1979). 'Environmental sociology: a framework for analysis' in T. O'Riordan and R. C. D'Arge (eds.), pp.57–85, Wiley, Chichester.

Dunlap, R. E. and Dillman, D. A. (1976). 'Decline in public support for environmental protection: evidence from 1970–1974 Panel Study', *Rur. Soc.*, **41**, 382–390.

Dunlap, R. E. and Van Liere, K. D. (1977a). 'Declining public support for environmental protection: "ecological backlash" or "natural decline".' Paper presented to Annual Meeting of the Rural Sociological Society, September, Scientific Paper No. 4804, Washington State University.

Dunlap, R. E. and Van Liere, K. D. (1977b). 'Further evidence of declining public concern with environmental problems: a research note', *Western Soc. Rev.*, **8**, 108–112.

Dunlap, R. E. and Van Liere, K. D. (1978a). 'The "new environmental paradigm"', *J. Environ. Educ.*, **9**, 10–19.

Dunlap, R. E. and Van Liere, K. D. (1978b). 'Commitment to the dominant social paradigm and support for ecological policies.' Paper presented to 1978 Annual Meeting of the Society for the Study for Social Problems.

Dunlap, R. E., Van Liere, K. D., and Dillman, D. A. (1979). 'Evidence of decline in public concern with environmental quality: a reply', *Rur. Soc.*, **44**, 204–212.

Durkheim, E. (1912). *The Elementary Forms of the Religious Life*, George Allen and Unwin, London.

Easlea, B. (1973). *Liberation and the Aims of Science: An Essay on Obstacles to the Building of a Beautiful World*, Chatto and Windus for Sussex University Press, London.

Easton, D. (1965). *A Systems Analysis of Political Life*, Wiley, New York.

The Ecologist, (1972). *A Blueprint for Survival*, Penguin, Harmondsworth.

Ehrenreich, B. and Ehrenreich, J. (1979). 'The professional–managerial class' in J. Walker (ed.), *Between Capital and Labour*, pp.5–45, Harvester Press, London.

Eiduson, B. T. (1962). *Scientists: Their Psychological World*, Basic Books, New York.

Elliott, D. and Elliott, R. (1976). *The Control of Technology*, Wykeham, London.

Ellul, J. (1965). *The Technological Society*, Jonathan Cape, London.

Encel, S. *et al.* (1975). *The Art of Anticipation: Values and Methods in Forecasting*, Martin Robertson, London.

Engels, F. (1969). 'Socialism: utopian and scientific' in L. S. Feuer (ed.), *Marx and Engels*, Fontana Library, London.

Enzensberger, H. M. (1974). 'A critique of political ecology', *New Left Rev.* **84**, 2–30.

Etzioni, A. (1961). *A Comparative Analysis of Complex Organizations*, Free Press, New York.

Fendrich, J. M. (1974). 'Activists ten years later: a test of generational unit continuity', *J. Social Issues*, **30**, 95–118.

Fendrich, J. M. and Tarleau, T. (1973). 'Marching to a different drummer: occupational and political correlates of former student activists', *Social Forces*, **52**, 245–253.

Feuer, L. S. (1969). *Marx and Engels*, Fontana, London.

Fietkau, H.-J. (1977). 'Environmental consciousness in Berlin', unpublished working paper.

Flacks, R. (1971). 'The revolt of the young intelligentsia: revolutionary class consciousness in post-scarcity America' in R. Aya and N. Miller (eds.), *The New American Revolution*, Collier Macmillan, London.

Flood, M. and Grove-White, R. (1976). *Nuclear Prospects: A Comment on the Individual, The State and Nuclear Power*, Friends of the Earth, London.

Fowles, J. (1977). 'The problem of values in futures research', *Futures*, **9**, 303–314.

Freidson, E. (ed.) (1973). *The Professions and Their Prospects*, Sage, Beverly Hills and London.

Friedland, E. I. (1974). 'Utopia and the science of the possible', *Polity*, **7**,

Galbraith, J. K. (1962). *The Affluent Society*, Penguin, Harmondsworth.

Galbraith, J. K. (1972). *The New Industrial State* (rev. edn), Andre Deutsch, London.

Galbraith, J. K. (1974). *Economics and the Public Purpose*, Andrew Deutsch.

Gale, R. P. (1980). 'The environmental movement and the left: preliminary considerations'. Paper to Pacific Sociological Association.

Gellner, E. (1975). 'A social contract in search of an idiom: the demise of the Danegeld State?', *Pol. Quart.*, **46**, 127–152.

George, D. (1953). *England in Transition*, Penguin, Harmondsworth.

Gershuny, J. (1978). *After Industrial Society?: The Emerging Self-Service Economy*, Macmillan, London.

Gerth, H. H. and Mills, C. W. (1948). *From Max Weber: Essays in Sociology*, Routledge and Kegan Paul, London.

Giddens, A. (1973). *The Class Structure of the Advanced Societies*, Hutchinson, London.

Goffman, E. (1969). *Where the Action Is*, Allen Lane, London.

Goldsmith, E. (1974). 'The ecology of war', *The Ecologist*, **4**, 125.

Goldsmith, E. *et al.* (1972). *A Blueprint for Survival*, Penguin, Harmondsworth.

Goldsmith, E. *et al.* (1978). 'Reprocessing the truth', *The Ecologist*, Spring.

Goldthorpe, J. H. *et al.* (1968). *The Affluent Worker: Industrial Attitudes and Behaviour*, University Press, Cambridge.

Gouldner, A. W. (1979). *The Future of Intellectuals and the Rise of the New Class*, Macmillan, London.

Gramsci, A. (1971). *Selections from the Prison Notebooks*, International Publishers, New York.

Gregory, R. (1971). *The Price of Amenity*, Macmillan, London.

Griffiths, R. F. (ed.) (1981). *Dealing with Risk: The Planning, Management and Acceptability of Technological Risk*, Manchester University Press.

Habermas, J. (1971). *Toward a Rational Society: Student Protest, Science and Politics*, Heinemann, London.

Habermas, J. (1976). 'Systematically distorted communication' and 'Problems of legitimation in late capitalism', in P. Connerton (ed.), *Critical Sociology*, Penguin, Harmondsworth.

Halmos, P. (ed.) (1973). *Professionalisation and Social Change*, Soc. Rev. Mono. 20.

Hardin, G. (1968). 'Tragedy of the commons', *Science*, **162**, 1243–2348.

Hardin, G. (1974). 'The economics of wilderness', *The Ecologist*, Vol. 4, no. 3.

Harper, P. (1974). 'What's left of alternative technology', *Undercurrents*, No. 6.

Heilbronner, R. L. (1976). *Business Civilisation in Decline*, Marion Bojors, London.

Herzberg, F. (1968). *Work and the Nature of Man*, Staples Press, London.

Hilderbrandt, K. and Dalton, R. J. (1978). 'New politics: political change or sunshine politics' in M. Kaase, and K. Von Beyme (eds.) *Elections and Parties*, Sage Publications, London.

Holton, G. (1974). 'On being caught between Dionysians and Apollonians', *Daedalus*, **103**, 65–81.

Inglehart, R. (1977). *The Silent Revolution: Changing Values and Political Styles among Western Publics*, Princeton University Press.

Inhaber, H. (n.d.). *Risk of Energy Production*, Atomic Energy Control Board, Ottawa.

Jahoda, M. (1973). 'Postscript on social change' in H. S. D. Cole *et al.* (eds.), *Thinking About the Future: A Critique of the Limits to Growth*, pp.209–215, Chatto and Windus for Sussex University Press, London.

Jahoda, M. and Freeman, C. (ed.) (1978). *World Futures: The Great Debate*, Martin Robertson, Oxford.

Jennings, J. *et al.* (1979). 'Generations and families' in S. H. Barnes and M. Kaase (eds.), *Political Action: Mass Participation in Five Western Democracies*, Chapter 15, Sage, Beverly Hills and London.

Kaase, M. and Von Beyme, K. (eds.), (1978). *Elections and Parties*, Sage Publications, London, and *German Pol. Stud.*, **3**, 70–96.

Keller, J. A. (1971). 'Types of motives for ecological concern', *Zygon*, **6**, 197–209.

Kerr, C. *et al.* (1960). *Industrialism and Industrial Man*, Heinemann, London.

King, R. and Nugent, N., (eds) (1979). *Respectable Rebels: Middle Class Campaigns in Britain in the 1970s*, Hodder and Stoughton, London.

Kluckhohn, F. R. and Strodtbeck, F. L. (1961). *Variations in Value Orientations*, Row Peterson, Evanston, Illinois.

Koestler, A. (1972). *Beyond Reductionism*, Hutchinson, London.

Komarov, B. (1978). *The Destruction of Nature in the Soviet Union*, Pluto Press, London.

Kristol, I. (1979). 'The adversary culture of intellectuals', *Encounter*, **53**, 5–14.

Kuhn, T. S. (1970). *The Structure of Scientific Revolutions* (2nd edn.), Chicago University Press.

Kumar, K. (1978). *Prophecy and Progress*, Penguin, Harmondsworth.

Landes, D. S. (1969). *The Unbound Prometheus*, University Press, Cambridge.

Laslett, P. (1965). *The World We Have Lost*, Methuen, London.

Leiss, W. (1972). *The Domination of Nature*, George Braziller, New York.

Lindberg, L. N. (ed.) (1976). *Politics and the Future of Industrial Society*, David McKay, New York.

Lipset, S. M. (1963). *Political Man*, Heinemann, London.

Lipset, S. M. (1980). 'The tax revolt and the welfare state', *New Soc.* **54**, 72–73.

Logan, R., and Nelkin, D. (1980). 'Labor and nuclear power', *Environment*, **22**, 6–34.

Lowe, P., Clifford, J., and Buchanan, S. (1980). 'The mass movement of the decade', *Vole*, **1**, 26–28.

Lowe, P. D. and Worboys, M. W. (1980). 'Ecology and ideology', in F. H. Buttel and H. N. Newby (eds.), *Sociology of Advanced Societies*, pp.433–452, Croom Helm, London.

Maddox, J. (1972). *The Doomsday Syndrome*, Macmillan, London.

Mann, M. (1970). 'The social cohesion of liberal democracy', *Amer. Soc. Rev.*, **35**, 423–439.

Mannheim, K. (1953). *Essays on Sociology and Social Psychology*, Routledge and Kegan Paul, London.

Mannheim, K. (1966). *Ideology and Utopia*, Routledge and Kegan Paul, London.

Marsh, A. (1977). *Protest and Political Consciousness*, Sage, London.

Marsh, A. (1980). 'Environmental issues in contemporary European politics'. Paper at 49th Nobel Symposium, The European Transition Away from Oil, Stockholm, April.

Marstrand, P. K. and Sinclair, T. C. 'The pollution sub-system' in H. S. D. Cole *et al.* (eds.), *Thinking About the Future: A Critique of the Limits to Growth*, pp.80–89, Chatto and Windus for Sussex University Press, London.

McKennell, A. C. (1977). 'Attitude scale construction' in C. A. O'Muircheartaigh, and C. Payne (eds.), *The Analysis of Survey Data*, Vol. 1, pp.183–220, Wiley, London.

Meadows, D. H. *et al.* (1972). *The Limits to Growth*, Earth Island, London.

Medawar, P. (1969). *Induction and Intuition in Scientific Thought*, Methuen, London.

Mesarovic, M. and Pestel, E. (1975). *Mankind at the Turning Point: The Second Report to the Club of Rome*, Hutchinson, London.

Milbrath, L. W. (1975). *Environmental Beliefs: A Tale of Two Counties*, Mimeographed Report, State University of New York at Buffalo.

Mishan, E. J. (1967). *The Costs of Economic Growth*, Staples Press, London.

Mitchell, R. C. (1978). 'The public speaks again: a new environmental survey', *Resources for the Future*, **60**, 1–6.

Mitchell, R. C. (1980). 'How "soft", "deep", or "left"?: present constituencies in the environmental movement for certain world views', *Nat. Res. J.*, **20**, 345–358.

Monod, J. (1971). *Chance and Necessity: An Essay on the Natural Philosophy of Modern Biology*, Alfred A. Knopf, New York.

Morrison, D. E., and Dunlap, R. E. (1980). 'Elitism, equality and environmentalism', Mimeo:— Department of Sociology, Michigan State University.

Mulkay, M. (1979). *Science and the Sociology of Knowledge*, George Allen and Unwin, London.

Nelkin, D. (1975). 'The political impact of technical expertise', *Soc. Stud. Sci.*, **5**, 35–54.

Nelkin, D. (1977). *Technological Decisions and Democracy*, Sage Publications, London.

Nelkin, D. and Pollak, M. (1980a). 'Ideology as strategy: the discourse of the anti-nuclear movement in France and Germany', *Sci., Tech. Hum. Values*, **5**, 3–13.

Nelkin, D. and Pollak, M. (1980b). 'Political parties and the nuclear energy debate in France and Germany', *Comp. Pol.*, **12**, 127–141.

Nie, N. H. *et al.* (1975). *Statistical Package for the Social Sciences*, McGraw-Hill, New York.

Nisbet, R. A. (1970). *The Sociological Tradition*, Heinemann, London.

Noble, T. (1978). 'Social Choice in Machine Design', *Politics and Soc.*, **8**, 321–338.

Nordhoff, C. (1966). *The Communistic Societies of the United States*, Dover Publications, New York.

Nowell-Smith, P. H. (1954). *Ethics*, Penguin Books, Harmondsworth.

Nowotny, H. (1977). 'Scientific purity and the nuclear danger: a case of risk assessment' in E. Mendelsohn, P. Weingart, and R. Whitley (eds.), *The Social Production of Scientific Knowledge*, D. Reidel, Dordrecht.

Odum, E. P. (1971). *Fundamentals of Ecology* (3rd edn), W. B. Saunders, Philadelphia.

O'Riordan, T. (1976). *Environmentalism*, Pion, London.

O'Riordan, T. (1979). 'Public interst environmental groups in the United States and Britain', *Amer. Stud.*, **13** (3), 409–438.

O'Riordan, T., and D'Arge, R. C. (1979). *Progress in Resource Management and Environmental Concern*, Wiley, Chichester.

Osgood, C. E. *et al.*, (1959). *The Measurement of Meaning*, Illinois University Press.

Otway, H. J., Maurer, D., and Thomas, K. (1978). 'Nuclear power: the question of public acceptance', *Futures*, **10**, 109–118.

Page, W. (1973). 'The population sub-system' in H. S. D. Cole *et al.* (eds.), *Thinking About the Future: A Critique of the Limits to Growth*, pp.43–55, Chatto and Windus for Sussex University Press, London.

Pahl, R. E. and Winkler, J. T. (1974). 'The coming corporatism', *New Society*, **30**, 72–76.

Parker, Mr. Justice, (1978). *The Windscale Enquiry*, H.M.S.O., London.

Parkin, F. (1968). *Middle Class Radicalism*, Manchester University Press.

Parkin, F. (1971). *Class Inequality and Political Order*, MacGibbon and Kee, London.

Parkin, F. (1979). *Marxism and Class Theory: A Bourgeois Critique*, Tavistock Publications, London.

Passmore, J. (1974). 'Removing the rubbish', *Encounter*, **42**, 11–24.

Pearce, A. W. (1979). 'World energy prospects', *Esso Magazine*, **11**, 3–4.

Pearce D. (1973). 'Is ecology elitist?', *Ecologist*, February, 61–63.

Pflemic, B. (1979). *Legitimacy and the Nuclear Energy Debate*, unpublished undergraduate dissertation, Polytechnic of North London.

Pirages, D. C. (1977). 'Introduction, a social design for sustainable growth' in D. C. Pirages (ed.), *The Sustainable Society: Implications for Growth* pp.1–13, Praeger Publications, New York and London.

Plant, R. (1979). *Community and Ideology*, Routledge and Kegan Paul, London.

Pocock, C. C. (1978). *A Fast-Changing World—The Political Challenge*, paper read at the Seventh World Planning Congress, September, London.

Poggi, G. (1978). *The Development of the Modern State*, Hutchinson University Library, London.

Polanyi, M. (1958). *Personal Knowledge: Towards a Post-Critical Philosophy*, Routledge and Kegan Paul, London.

Popper, K. R. (1945). *The Open Society and Its Enemies: Vol. 1, The Spell of Plato*, Routledge and Kegan Paul, London.

Poulantzas, N. (1975). *Classes in Contemporary Capitalism*, New Left Books, London.

Reich, C. (1971). *The Greening of America*, Penguin, Harmondsworth.

Rescher, N. (1978). *Scientific Progress*, Basil Blackwell, Oxford.

Richter, P. E. (1971). *Utopias: Social Ideals and Communal Experiments*, Holbrook Press, Boston.

Rigby, A. (1974). *Alternative Realities: A Study of Communes and their Members*, Routledge and Kegan Paul, London.

Rokeach, M. (1973). *The Nature of Human Values*, Free Press, New York.

Rokeach, M. (1974). 'Change and stability in American value systems 1968–1971' *Pub. Opin. Quart.*, **38**, 222–238.

Room, G. J. (1979). *The Sociology of Welfare: Social Policy, Stratification and Political Order*, Martin Robertson, Oxford.

Rose, A. M. (ed.) (1962). *Human Behaviour and Social Processes*, Routledge and Kegan Paul, London.

Rose, H. and Rose, S. (1974). '"Do not adjust your mind, there is a fault in reality": ideology in the neurobiological sciences' in R. Whitley (ed.), *Social Processes of Scientific Development*, pp.148–171, Routledge and Kegan Paul, London.

Rose, M. (1979). *Servants of Post-Industrial Power?*, Macmillan, London.

Rosenberg, M. *et al.*, (1958). *Occupations and Values*, Free Press, Glencoe, Illinois.

Ross, G. (1978). 'Marxism and the new middle classes: French critiques', *Theory and Soc.*, **5**, 163–190.

Roszak, T. (1970). *The Making of a Counter Culture: Reflections on the Techno-cratic Society and its Youthful Opposition*, Faber and Faber, London.

Roszak, T. (1972). *Where the Wasteland Ends: Politics and Transcendence in Post-Industrial Society*, Doubleday, New York.

Rothman, H. (1972). *Murderous Providence*, Rupert Hart-Davis, London.

Rothschild, Lord. (1978). 'Risk', *The Listener*, 30 November, 715–718.

Royal Commission on Environmental Pollution, (1976). *Sixth Report: Nuclear Power and the Environment*, Cmnd. 6618, H.M.S.O., London.

Sandbach, F. (1980). *Environment, Ideology and Policy*, Blackwell, Oxford.

Schnaiberg, A. (1980). *The Environment: From Surplus to Scarcity*, Oxford University Press.

Science and Society, Council for, (1977). *The Acceptability of Risk*, Barry Rose, London.

Sherman, B. (1972). 'Environmentalists and workers unite!', *Your Environment*, **3**, 10–12.

Sibley, M. Q. (1973). 'Utopian thought and technology', *Amer. J. Pol. Sci.* **17**, 255–281.

Simmons, H. G. (1973). 'System dynamics and technocracy' in H. S. D. Cole *et al.* (eds.) *Thinking About the Future: A Critique of the Limits to Growth*, pp.192–208, Chatto and Windus for Sussex University Press, London.

Sinclair, T. C. (1973). 'Environmentalism' in H. S. D. Cole *et al.* (eds.), *Thinking About the Future: A Critique of the Limits to Growth*, pp.175–191, Chatto and Windus for Sussex University Press, London.

Skinner, B. (1948). *Walden Two*, Macmillan, New York.

Skolimowski, H. (1978). 'Eco-philosophy versus the scientific world view' *The Eco. Quart.*, **3**, 227–241.

Smelser, N. J. (1962). *Theory of Collective Behaviour*, Routledge and Kegan Paul, London.

Stretton, H. (1976). *Capitalism, Socialism and the Environment*, University Press, Cambridge.

Surrey, J., and Huggett, C. (1976). 'Opposition to nuclear power: a review of international experience', *Energy Pol.*, **4**, 286–307.

Tallman, I. and Ihinger-Tallman, M. (1979). 'Values, distributive justice and social change', *Amer. Rev. Soc.*, **44**, 216–235.

Tanzer, M. (1974). *The Energy Crisis: World Struggle for Power and Wealth*, Monthly Review Press, New York and London.

Taylor, R. and Pritchard, C. (1980). *The Protest Makers: The British Nuclear Disarmament Movement of 1958–1965 Twenty Years On*, Pergamon Press, Oxford.

Thomas, W. I. and Znaniecki, F. (1958). *The Polish Peasant in Europe And America* (2nd edn), Dover, New York.

Thompson, M. (1978). 'Risk and restriction in nuclear society'. Unpublished working paper.

Thompson, M. (1979a). *Rubbish Theory: The Creation and Destruction of Values*, Oxford University Press.

Thompson, M. (1979b). 'Sahibs and Sherpas', *Mountain*, **68**, 45–49.

Tonnies, F. (1955). *Community and Association*, Routledge and Kegan Paul, London.

Touraine, A. (1979). 'Political ecology: a demand to live differently now', *New Society*, 8 November, pp.307–309.

Trilling, L. (1961). *Beyond Culture: Essays on Literature and Learning*, Secker and Warburg, London.

Van Liere, K. D., and Dunlap, R. E. (1980). 'The social bases of environmental concern: a review of hypotheses, explanations and empirical evidence', *Pub. Opin. Quart.*, **44**, 181–197.

Walker, P. (ed.) (1979). *Between Capital and Labour*, Harvester Press, London.
Warner, F. (1981). 'Foreword: The foundations of risk assessment' in R. F. Griffiths (ed.), *Dealing with Risk: The Planning, Management and Acceptability of Technological Risk*, p.xii, Manchester University Press.
Weber, M. (1930). *The Protestant Ethic and the Spirit of Capitalism*, George Allen and Unwin, London.
Weber, M. (1968). *Economy and Society*, Bedminster Press, New York.
Weiner, M. J. (1981). *English Culture and the Decline of the Industrial Spirit*, Cambridge University Press.
Westergaard, J. and Resler, H. (1975). *Class in Capitalist Society*, Heinemann, London.
White, L. Jr. (1967). 'The historical roots of our ecological crisis', *Science*, **155**, 1203–1207.
Whitehead, A. N. (1967). *Science in the Modern World*, Free Press, Illinois.
Williams, R. (1972). 'Ideas of Nature' in J. Benthall (ed.), *Ecology, The Shaping Enquiry*, Longman, London.
Woodcock, G. (1974). 'Anarchism and ecology', *Ecologist*, **4**, 84–88.
Wright, E. D. (1979). 'Intellectuals and the class structure of capitalist society' in P. Walker (ed.), *Between Capital and Labour*, Chapter 7, Harvester Press, London.

Index

adolescence, 53
age:
    and environmentalists, 19, 137
    and environmental concern, 133, 134
alternative:
    beliefs and values, 37
    futures, 101–121
    paradigms, 117
    styles of thought, 62–66
    technology, 7
    utopias, 5–7
anarchist tradition, 60, 103
autonomy, 42, 60

Big Men, 40–43
Blueprint For Survival, 1, 3, 8
blueprintism, 103
bourgeois culture, 111
bourgeoisie, 64, 94
bureaucracy, 60–61, 70
bureaucratic apparatus, 71
business civilization, 110
business culture, 49–52, 61, 91

cash nexus, 59, 69
Catastrophists, 25, 26, 119–120
capitalism, 56, 59, 66, 69, 95, 110, 117
capitalist mode of production, 67
castes, 41–42
centralization, 75
civil rights, 22
civil servants, 43
class, 61–62
    dominant, 107
    functionalist theories of, 61
    ruling, 94, 106
    middle, 19, 34, 52, 77, 115

    new middle, 93–97
Club of Rome, 1, 3, 103
coalitions, 90, 93, 112–114
communication:
    political, 89, 97–98
community, 59–60
CND (Campaign for Nuclear Disarmament), 21, 45, 74, 76, 77
conflict, 69–70
Conservation Society, 3, 14
constituencies, 112–114
Cornucopians, 119–120
corporatism, 75
cosmologies:
    and environments, 39–43
cost–benefit analysis, 87–88
counter-culture, 58, 61, 72
Cow Green reservoir, 86
cultural contexts, 25, 82
culture:
    and society, 52–53, 111
    business, 49–52
    crisis of, 109–112

decentralized, 61
democracy, 69–70
depoliticization, 75, 98, 119
Dionysian, 64
direct action, 74, 76–80, 118
division of labour, 60
dominant class, 107
dominant social paradigm, 27–32, 88
domination, 63
Durkheim, 59, 70

ecological:
    backlash, 9

151